The Smestow
Wolverhampton's River

Angus Dunphy OBE

The Black Country Society

The term 'The Black Country' was coined in the mid-19th Century to describe that area of the South Staffordshire coalfield where the 'thick coal' lay.

Over 150 square miles some 100 small industrial communities developed and by the late 1890s a couple of dozen of them were of sufficient size, perhaps when linked with some of their neighbours, to have their own local councils. Since that time there have been several local government reorganisations and after that of 1974 all of the townships of the Black Country were absorbed into the four Black Country Metropolitan Boroughs of Dudley, Sandwell, Walsall and Wolverhampton. In December 2000 Wolverhampton was granted city status.

The Black Country Society was founded in 1967 by enthusiasts, led by Dr John Fletcher, who felt that the Black Country did not receive its fair share of recognition for its great contribution to the industrial development of Britain and the world.

The Society grew out of the Dudley Canal Trust Preservation Society which had successfully campaigned to save Dudley Canal Tunnel which had been threatened with closure by the British Waterways Board and British Rail. The preserved tunnel linking the Birmingham Canal System and the canals of the Stour Valley, with links to the River Severn, is now a major attraction at the Black Country Living Museum.

The stated aim of the Society is to *"foster interest in the past, present and future of the Black Country"*. Its voice calling for the establishment of a local industrial museum at a meeting on 6 October 1968 was one of the first on the subject.

The Black Country Society produces a high quality, quarterly magazine, The Blackcountryman. It began publication in 1967 and has evolved throughout the years to become a well-respected publication. The Society also hold meetings, talks, trips and walks in the Black Country and welcome members and non-members to its talks, to take part in other activities requires membership.

Membership is very reasonably priced, more details can be obtained from the Society website: **www.blackcountrysociety.co.uk**. The Society has also published many books on the Black Country, many of these are available via the website and at outlets throughout the Black Country.

For further details email the editior, Mike Pearson: editor@blackcountrysociety.co.uk.

Acknowledgements

A book such as this is dependent upon the goodwill, guidance and support of many people, and this is certainly true in this case.

I first want to mention the cartographers: Jenny Denton of Swansea, David Leverton of Dinas Powys, and Jeanette Jones of Llandovery. Their spatial awareness adds much to support the text.

I am most grateful to Dr Peter King of Hagley and May Griffiths MBE, the Wombourne historian, for their support in acting as critical friends and for supplying additional information.

As always I have found the people of South Staffordshire generous in allowing me access to their property and for giving me time and information. I particularly wish to thank Mr and Mrs Frank Edwards of Mill Farm, Spittlebrook; Mr Charles Wilkes of Checkhill Farm; Mr Roger Pearson of Smestow Watermill; Mr David and Mrs Vee Hingley of Himley Mill. I am indebted to Mr and Mrs Peter Williams of Enville Estates for their exceptional kindness in allowing me to visit Mere Mill, and I am grateful for the support that their staff gave me in arranging and providing access. The copyright of the photographs taken there by the skilful Mr Barrie Phillips lies with Enville Estates. Mrs Sandy Haynes of Enville Estate Archives, Mrs Liz Jukes of the Estate Office and Mr Geoffrey Smith, a direct descendent of the Toy family considerably helped me in my task.

Mr John and Mrs Carolyn Phillips of The Wombourne Wodehouse were kind enough to suggest alterations and additions to the Wodehouse Mill story found in Chapter 11. The late Mr Phillip Beards of Pennfields corresponded with me over many years and in this instance provided valuable information on the Graiseley Brook.

Every effort has been made to contact copyright holders of images, where copyright has not originated from those who own them. Ron Davies has allowed me to reproduce his sketch of the Wodehouse Mill wheel and the photographs of the Wodehouse Mill pool and Holbeche Mill, which has since vanished from our scene. The late Andrew Barnett has a number of his sketches in this volume. Apart from illustrating the text, they serve to remind me of our twice or thrice weekly lunch hour trips out into the countryside from our then respective Gornal schools. The sketches made were reproduced in various forms through the able services of the then warden of Dudley Teachers' Centre, Stan Hill, who was based in the ex laundry block behind Himley Hall. He has remained a great friend and adviser and I am ever grateful for his support with this book. Stan continues to promote the writing of local history in the Black Country and its green borderland. David Leverton has provided three sketches – those of Oxley and the Stour Valley railway viaducts and the scene at Seisdon Mill. Harry and Ann Brown supplied the excellent photographs of Trysull Mill at the time of the Summertons, whilst John Fanshaw of Dinas Powys provided a couple of photographs of the lower reaches of the Smestow. I purchased the sketch book of Frank Sproson many years ago and I have used several of his ink drawings such as that of Wightwick Mill and the Lock House. Sale catalogues such as those of the Prestwood Estate in 1913, the southern portions of the Wrottesley Estate in 1929 and the Himley Estate sale of 1947 have provided a number of useful images. A detail from South Staffordshire Water Company's 1909 excerpt of an OS 6-inch map shows the effects of Hinksford pumping station on village wells. I acknowledge Alan Wellings' sketch of the bridges at Newbridge, which appeared in Eustace Lees' epic poem The Smestow. Mrs Edwards contributed the old photographs of the mill at Spittlebrook. Mr John Sparry, raconteur, historian, musician and book dealer, lent me Fowler's Kingswinford map.

Writing a book is one thing, preparing it for print is entirely another activity. David Leverton designed the volume and did the initial typesetting. I pay tribute to his commitment and resolve. Mike Pearson, the editor of The Blackcountryman is responsible for getting the book ready for printing and for seeing it through that process. Without these two gentlemen there would be no book.

If I have failed to thank others please accept my sincere apologies, for you too will have had a hand in its text. And finally I must thank my wife, Gail, and friends for their company on our walks through Smestow Country.

Angus Dunphy OBE
Dinas Powys
October, 2012

Dedication

FOR SOUTH STAFFORDSHIRE LOCAL HISTORIANS

and in particular:

The late Andrew Barnett
– The ancient Manor of Sedgley

Geoffrey Hancock
– Tettenhall

Stan Hill
Founder Warden of Dudley Teachers' Centre and one-time editor of The Blackcountryman
– Brierley Hill and The Black Country

May Griffiths MBE
– The Parish of Wombourne with Swindon and Orton Liberties

Tony Unwin
– The Parishes of Seisdon and Trysull

Contents

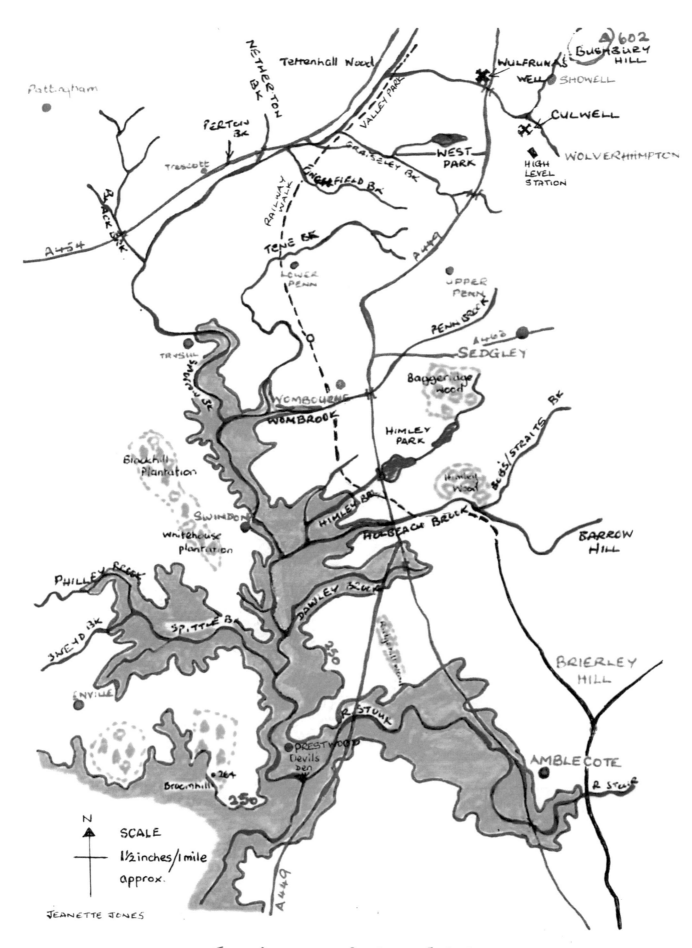

Fig. 1 THE SMESTOW BROOK SYSTEM

Introduction

Little has been written about the Smestow Brook and there is no definitive work on the subject. This book is a first attempt to rectify the matter. It has been five years in preparation, the author taking odd moments to research a further aspect or two, much like laying the next course of bricks on a wall. At this stage I thought I had better get something in print, before what beats us all – the passage of time – wins.

Wolverhampton lies astride the great central watershed of England. It is drained by the headwaters of three principal streams. The Penk, which rises on the Tettenhall plateau, and the Black Country Tame flow to join the Trent and hence the North Sea. The Smestow on the other hand swings south to swell the Stour at Prestwood, the waters eventually reaching the Severn and the Bristol Channel. The town, or city as it now is, could in theory have acquired the name of Wolverhampton on Penk or Tame and rivalled the Newcastles, Stokes, Kingstons of this country. It might even have been called Wolverhampton on Smestow. In the event it was proud to bear the name of Wulfruna's High Town.

The Smestow's drainage basin was created after the last ice age. Prior to this its headwaters flowed north and were part of the Penk system. Thomas Kitchen's map of 1722 shows one of the earliest schemes for a canal in England. It proposed a waterway linking the headwaters of the Smestow at Newbridge, with those of the Penk at Pendeford Mill. This was virtually the route followed by the Staffordshire and Worcestershire Canal Navigation half a century later. The map highlights Wolverhampton's watershed location.

Fig. 2
Proposed waterway linking Smestow with Penk, 1722

This book traces the route taken by the Smestow and its tributaries and comments on a range of features that lie along, or near to its banks. The main stream is but thirteen miles long (1). However, there are several major tributaries, many of which fall sharply from the South Staffordshire plateau, or from the Enville district, thus creating the potential for harnessing the available water power. Man was not lacking in this regard historically, using it to drive plant for the fulling of cloth, the milling of grain, the bellows of a charcoal blast furnace and the hammers of blade mills, forges and ironworks. The number of industrial sites is simply staggering.

The scene today is very different as we appear to have turned our back on water power in this region. The Wodehouse Mill was the last in the district to work, grinding corn for cattle feed until 1976. After milling had ceased over the period between 1880 and 1920, a few mills used water power to generate electricity for their farms, but even this had ceased by the end of the 1930s. Opportunity exists, if we are inventive, to use the natural resource of water in a variety of ways, which could include electricity generation, irrigation, fire safety measures and ensuring the water table is kept at a reasonable level. Strong financial support would be an essential ingredient for any scheme. Only then will we follow in the footsteps of those who have gone before, in harnessing the Smestow.

The Smestow Brook and its tributaries flow through some of the loveliest countryside, so sit back and read on – and enjoy the journey.

(1) *The Staffordshire Encyclopaedia, Tim Cockin, 2000, P522.*

Key to map (right)

No.	Name	Grid ref	No.	Name	Grid ref
1	SHOWELL MILL	SJ 925009 ?	20	HOLLOW MILL	SO 865899
2	GORSE BROOK MILL	SJ 914005	21	HINKSFORD FORGE	SO 868898
3	DUNSTALL MILL	SJ 902003	22	HINKSFORD FARM MILL	SO 869901
4	COMPTON MILL	SO 883990	23	HIMLEY MILL	SO 878911
5	WIGHTWICK MILL	SO 875983	24	HIMLEY FURNACE	SO 890916
6	PERTON MILL	SO 858977	25	WALL HEATH FORGE	SO 875901
7	GRANGE FURNACE	SO 844965	26	HOLBEACH MILL	SO 884905
	FURNACE GRANGE MILL		27	OAK MILL	SO 893907
	TRESCOTT MILL	SO 850967 ?	28	COPPICE MILL	SO 903906
8	GREAT MOOR MILL	SO 837984	29	HASCO(D) FURNACE	SO 902909
9	SEISDON MILL	SO 839948	30	COTWALLEND MILL	SO 912927
10	TRYSULL MILL	SO 851944	31	GORNAL FORGE	SO 910901
11	SMESTOW MILL	SO 856916	32	HUNTS MILL	SO 914899
12	ORTON MILL	SO 868942 ?	33	GORNALWOOD FURNACE	?
13	PENN COMMON MILL	SO 895941 ?	34	GREENSFORGE (FORGE + MILL)	SO 861887
14	LUDE MILL	SO 888940 ?	35	GOTHERSLEY MILL (IRON WORKS)	SO 863869
15	WODEHOUSE MILL	SO 886938	36	CHECKHILL MILL	SO 856878
16	WOMBOURNE MILL	SO 878929	37	SPITTLE BROOK MILL	SO 845877
17	HAM MILL	SO 874928	38	HOO FARM MILL	SO 832878
18	HEATH FORGE	SO 858923	39	MORFE HALL FARM MILL	SO 829877
	HEATH MILL		40	MERE MILL	SO 822886
19	SWINDON FORGE	SO 862906	41	LUTLEY MILL	SO 818882
	SWINDON MILL		42	PHILLEY BROOK MILL	SO 812881
	SWINDON IRONWORKS		43	TOYS FARM MILL	SO 805875

8

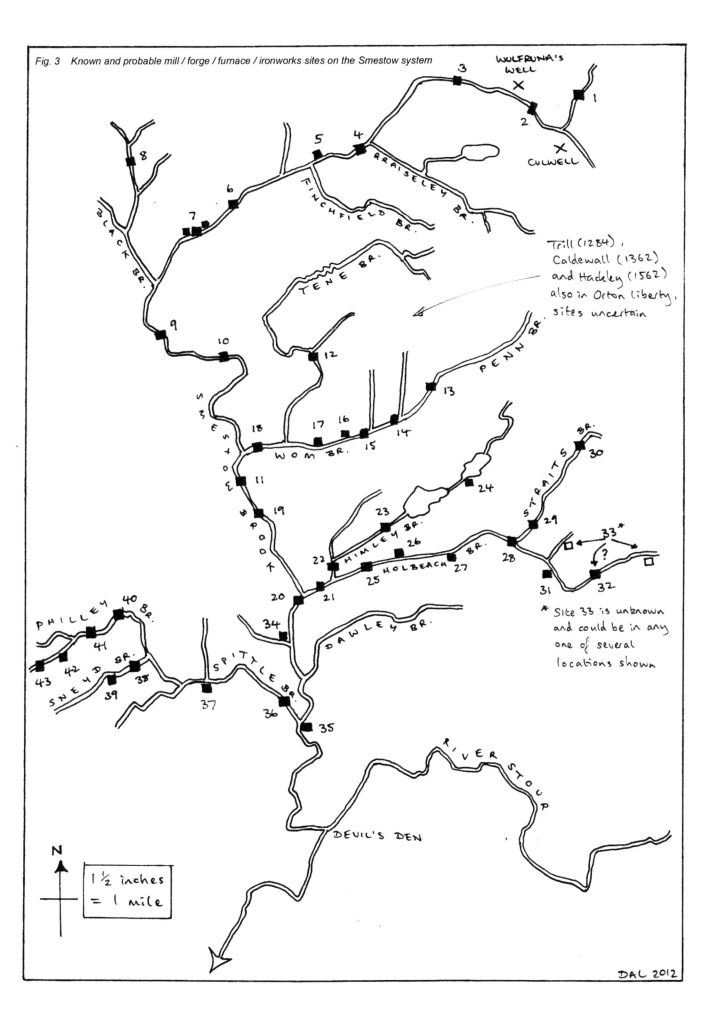

Fig. 3   Known and probable mill / forge / furnace / ironworks sites on the Smestow system

Trill (1284), Caldewall (1362) and Hadley (1562) also in Orton liberty, sites uncertain

* Site 33 is unknown and could be in any one of several locations shown

DAL 2012

1½ inches = 1 mile

The earliest known name for the Smestow is the Tresel. The same word stem is found in the village names of Trescott and Trysull, which lie further downstream. The word is Celtic, and means a river which swirls and toils. This is a very apt description of the physical characteristics of the stream. In fact, the few remaining Celtic place names in our district usually refer to landscape features: e.g. Penn, head of the hill; (Little) Onn, an ash tree; Cannock, a hill or high place; Kinver, the great ridge. On the other hand, Saxon names usually refer to settlement: e.g. Wolverhampton, Wulfruna's high town; Tettenhall, Tetta's hall or lookout place; Seisdon, the Saxon hill; Prestwood, the priest's wood.

Fig. 4

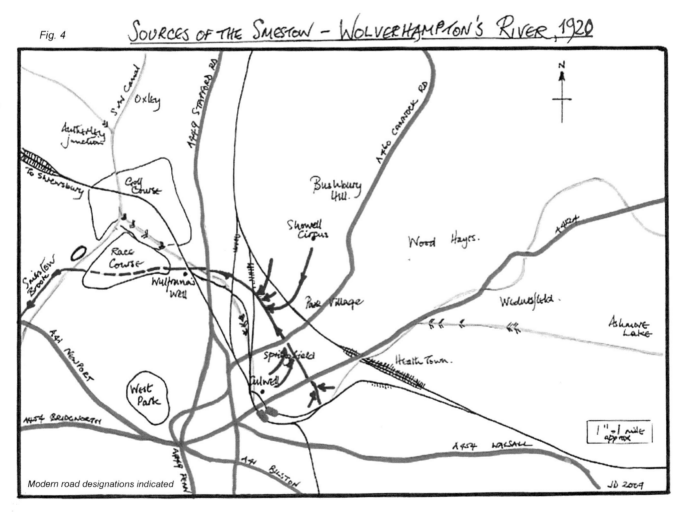

Sources of the Smestow – Wolverhampton's River, 1920

Modern road designations indicated

The Smestow's many sources can be viewed from the new bridge above platform 4 at Wolverhampton's railway station. Laid out at our feet is the area beyond the Wednesfield road, whilst to the left is St Stephen's Church and Springfield. In the far distance is Bushbury Hill, upon whose slopes one branch of the infant stream gathers strength. Seepages at Seawall, or Showell (probably meaning seven wells) *(1)*, filled the medieval moat and probably drove a farm corn mill. Legend attributes Lady Godiva as the owner of the Showell Estate, as well as the provider of the preaching cross at Penn Church. Both sites were of course connected by the Penway. In the seventeenth century the Huntbachs were the Showell's owners. Dugdale, the Herald, was connected to them by marriage. Showell Farm has gone, subsumed by the 1920s Low Hill Estate, but the memory is kept alive in the name Showell Circus. No longer does the brook tumble across the fields to Nine Elms Lane, for today much of its journey lies underground. Such is the price of progress.

The main branch begins life in the Inkerman/Alma Street/Causeway Lake district, beyond the Wednesfield Road and beneath the embankment of the Wolverhampton to Walsall railway. The rivulets flow underneath the Wednesfield Road towards the Cannock Road, across the district known as Springfield. In 1900 these were still the fields of Grimstone Farm, which was situated at the junction of Hilton Street and Cannock Road *(2)*. The waters are again swelled by springs, as the name implies. The Culwell, one of the city's earliest wells, was located where Culwell Street (Bridge Street) meets Wednesfield Road. It was no accident that William Butler built his brewery on land in Grimstone Street in 1873. He chose the spot because of the abundant supply of water, from springs and boreholes. Many would argue that this is what gave the ales their distinctive taste. Springfield Brewery closed in 1991 and was mourned by many for the loss of its beers and for the loss of its fine Victorian buildings, which have suffered from vandalism and fire *(3)*.

Fig. 5

Fig. 6 No. 5975 'Winslow Hall' passes Butler's Brewery with an express freight

The area so far covered was until very recent time a great hive of industry and included an iron works, foundry, lock maker, motor manufacturers, and engineering plants. These are some of the many trades which gave Wolverhampton its wealth. The town's motto, *'Out of darkness cometh light'* is very true. Interspersed amongst the factories were 19th and early 20th century domestic properties. This near city centre housing stock has been supplemented with the most modern of residences on the Whites Field area, between Springfield Road and Cannock Road.

The brook used to trickle down the sides of Whites Playing Fields, which were used as a second rugby pitch by Springfield Secondary Modern Boys' School until 1971 and for special events, such as the City's Boy Scout Annual Sports. On 1st July, 1950 Stan Cullis, the Wolves manager, opened them *(4)*. These were the golden years of this famous football club, with a 1949 cup final triumph still fresh in the memory of every boy. The waters coming from Springfield are piped under the Cannock Road, before running alongside Nine Elms Lane, where the Showell stream joins it. The waters, now swelled, cross Fowlers Park, named after Henry Hartley Fowler, the first Viscount Wolverhampton and one time Secretary of State for India, before reaching the gasworks site. Here in 1862 Henry Coxwell, a scientist, and James Glaisher, a professional balloonist, set a new world record in their balloon called Mammoth. They rose to a distance of seven miles as they studied the atmosphere. The balloon came down at Ludlow.

The Smestow Brook passes underneath the LNWR viaduct (Stour valley line) between the gas works and the site of the former Electric Construction Company, which made everything from transformers to switchgear between 1888 and the 1980s. Now quite a stream, the waters pass under the Stafford Road. Here was the Smestow's second watermill. Gorsebrook Mill is clearly shown on a map of 1766, which delineates the future course of the Birmingham Canal of 1772. This canal revolutionised trade and manufacture, for it promoted the economically efficient movement of manufactured wares, as well as of coal, the lifeblood of the Industrial Revolution. Gorsebrook Road and mill get their name

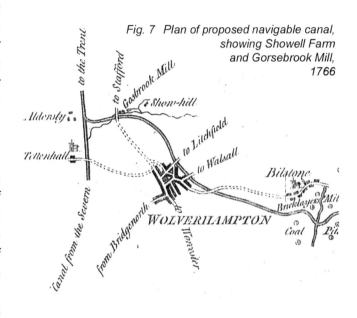

Fig. 7 Plan of proposed navigable canal, showing Showell Farm and Gorsebrook Mill, 1766

from the Goosebrook, the early name for this stretch of the Smestow. It is mentioned in Ethelred's Foundation Charter of 985 and marks the town's then boundary *(5)*. The brook flows westwards under the viaduct, as it heads for the racecourse.

On the other side of the Stafford Road is an exhibit of rails and a pair of locomotive wheels, which commemorate the Great Western Railway's presence in the city and the site of the nearby railway works. Wolverhampton was the headquarters of the railway's northern division. Its engine works made locomotives until 1908, and repaired them right up to closure in 1964. Nearby was Stafford Rd Engine Sheds, which prepared the crack expresses for London, Birkenhead and the Cambrian coast. Outside small boys abounded, collecting the names and numbers of King, Star, Saint, Castle and County class locomotives. Above us, crossing the Smestow Valley is Oxley Viaduct, which carries the tracks to Shrewsbury and beyond. It was the northern limit of Brunel's 7-foot gauge.

Fig. 8   OXLEY VIADUCT

13

Fig. 9 Wellhead, Wulfruna's Well

On the side of Dunstall Hill is Wulfruna's Well, named after the town's patron. She is believed to have endowed the monastery of St Mary's (now St Peter's) in 994. Michael Drayton in his *Polyolbion* of 1613 showed Wulfruna holding a pitcher of water at this spot, thus signifying his version of the river's source. He went further with these lines:

'Thus though th' industrious muse hath been imploy'd so long.
Yet is she loth to doe poore little Smestall wrong.
That from her Wilfune's Spring neere Hampton plyes to pour
The wealth shee there receives into her friendly Stour'
(6).

The wellhead was erected in 1901 by Alexander Staveley Hill QC, MP, one-time owner of Dunstall Park and Oxley Manor.

The Smestow flows, in part, underground along the southern fringes of the racecourse, towards the sites of Dunstall Hall and its medieval moat *(7)* and Dunstall Corn Mill. The seventeenth-century hall was demolished to make way for the Courtaulds plant of 1924/5. The factory, with its landmark chimneys (The Three Sisters), in turn has given way to the Farndale Housing Estate. The whole area of Whitmore Reans, which lies below the hills of Dunstall and the town centre, has traditionally been susceptible to flooding. The very

Fig. 10
·DUNSTALL·HALL·

name means the white (foggy?) moorland with drainage ditches. This area adds to the Smestow's waters.

Fig. 11 Tunstall Water Bridge

The Smestow Brook crosses underneath the racecourse, and re-emerging is carried by Tunstall Water Bridge over the Staffordshire and Worcestershire Canal at Aldersley. Aerial photographs taken in dry summers show its course. The canal company was careful to ensure an adequate supply of water for those mills and forges downstream, as it wished to avoid compensation payments.

There was once a footpath at this bridge, but access was stopped up to deny the public having an unpaid trip to the races. The City's first racecourse was at Broadmeadow, which became the West Park. The Staveley Hills sold Dunstall Park to the Racecourse Company in 1887. Here, in 1910 was held one of Britain's first flying meetings *(8)*. The weather was bad but flying did take place with all the famous names being present, CS Rolls, Cecil Grace, Captain Dawes, Lancelot Gibbs and Grahame White. White won the prize for the greatest amount of flying time over the four days, just fifteen minutes. The 1910 meeting represented a chapter in the early stages of aircraft development and flight.

At Aldersley the Smestow turns south.

(1) History of Wolverhampton, Mander and Tildesley, 1960, P9.
(2) Alan Godfrey's Old Ordnance Survey maps, Wolverhampton NE, 1901.
(3) Express and Star photograph and caption, August 3rd, 1991.
(4) Wolverhampton and District Boy Scouts sports programme, 1950.
(5) Copy issued by Wolverhampton Borough Council, 1985.
(6) ibid 1, P4.
(7) South Staffordshire Archaeological and Historical Society Volume 24, 1982- 3, P57.
(8) The Aero volume 3, no. 59, and Flight volume 2, no27.

Fig. 12   STOUR VALLEY VIADUCT

Fig. 13

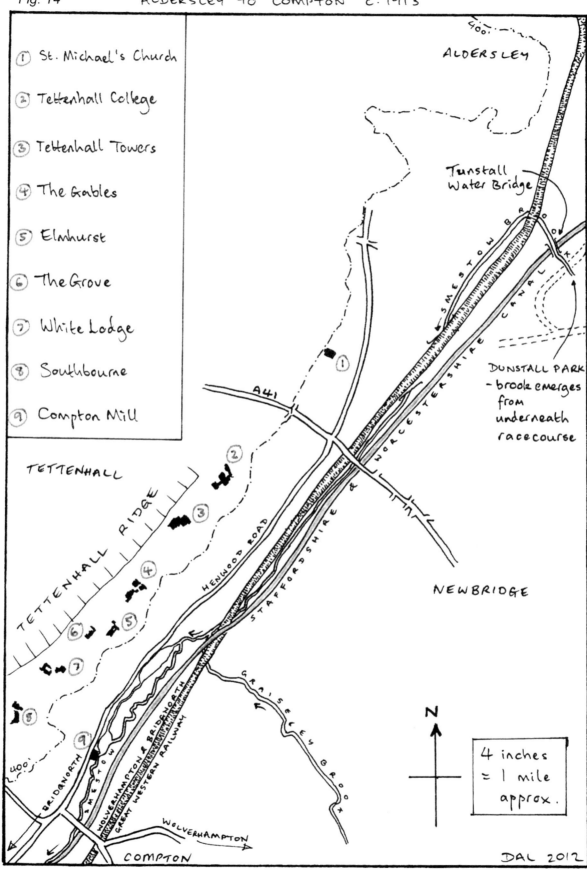

Fig. 14   ALDERSLEY TO COMPTON c. 1913

1. St. Michael's Church
2. Tettenhall College
3. Tettenhall Towers
4. The Gables
5. Elmhurst
6. The Grove
7. White Lodge
8. Southbourne
9. Compton Mill

DUNSTALL PARK - brook emerges from underneath racecourse

Tunstall Water Bridge

ALDERSLEY

NEWBRIDGE

TETTENHALL

N
4 inches = 1 mile approx.

DAL 2012

WOLVERHAMPTON
COMPTON

Between Aldersley and Tettenhall the Smestow Brook has been much culverted to reduce the risk of flooding. In 1955 pipes were laid near Aldersley Stadium, whilst forty years later 460 tons of soil was removed from under the Tettenhall Road to make room for 14 concrete pipes, each weighing 11 tons *(1)*. The tunnel replaced smaller conduits, one installed in the 1850s, and the other in the 1930s. Whitmore Reans, Dunstall Park and Tettenhall areas have benefited from the reduced risk of flooding and storm overflow from Barnhurst Sewage Farm. South of the Tettenhall Road the brook has been much regraded to assist with water flow.

The greatest visual impact of the river in this reach is not the man-made features associated with drainage, but the great cut made for it as it passes through the Tettenhall-Wightwick Gap. This was as a consequence of the main Irish Sea glaciation, which created the River Severn and its tributaries as we know them today. An ice dam to the north led to a build up of meltwater, which eventually overflowed, its erosive force carving out the features of the Tettenhall-Perton Ridge on the west and Finchfield Hill and Windmill Bank on the east. The modern eye often wrongly sees the insignificant Smestow as the culprit.

Early man must have used this natural routeway, keeping to the valley sides to avoid the marshy valley bottom. A Roman road runs from Watling Street at Stretton/Gailey to Greensforge Fort in the south. The line of it is lost between Pendeford and Hinksford, but a study of the map or the lie of the land suggests that the Romans would have used the Gap to travel south. They probably crossed the Smestow at Compton to march through Finchfield and Bradmore, before joining the line of the A449 at Lloyd Hill to reach the site of Wombourne Church and hence to Hinksford. Alternatively they could have continued to Wightwick or even Trescott, before crossing the stream and heading south.

Brindley's masterpiece, the Staffordshire and Worcestershire Canal Navigation of 1772 used the Smestow Valley, as did the Oxley Junction-Kingswinford Junction Railway between 1925 and 1965. In this stretch of their journey both keep the brook close company. The Valley Park, the railway's successor, offers the walker and rider excellent opportunities for outdoor leisure. It is also an important site for nature conservation and is protected by the environmental policies of the City of Wolverhampton's Development Plan. The kingfisher has returned, just one of a wide variety of birds which can be seen. Others include kestrels, finches, tits, redwings and even the goldcrest. A £600,000 redevelopment scheme to provide a new visitor centre at Tettenhall Railway Station was begun in January 2008. It is ideally situated at approximately halfway along Wolverhampton's 150-acre Smestow Valley Nature Reserve, which runs from Aldersley to Wightwick.

The year 910 saw the Battle of Tettenhall, and whilst the battlefield itself is lost in the mists of time and may well have been at Wednesfield, the Smestow Valley would have experienced the footsteps of the forces. The battle took place between a significant Danish raiding army trying to get back north to the Danelaw with their booty, and a Saxon force made up of Mercians and West Saxons. This may well have been in response to a Saxon force which had raided the Danelaw the previous year. On the return from their summer raid the Danes crossed the Severn at Quatford, possibly by a timber bridge and if not by the ford *(2)*. River levels may have been low. The Danes may well have travelled along the remains of the Roman road to Greensforge, which ran through Morfe Forest and via Broughton, Bobbington and Highgate Common. From Greensforge another Roman road led to Watling Street via Hinksford, the site of Wombourne Church and probably up onto the Orton Hills at Pickerills Hill. A straight route by way of Bearnett Lane, Showell Lane, Springhill Lane, Drivefields, Langley Road and the Bhylls leads to Wightwick and the Smestow Valley. Perhaps of mere coincidence are the sites of burial lows between Smestow Bridge and Trysull and that which was once near Wightwick Mill. They could represent a much earlier age. Wombourne, of course, has a Battlefield Hill and folklore claims this as the site of a skirmish. Whatever the route taken and whatever the sketchy evidence, there was a battle where three Danish Kings – Eowils, Halfdan and Inguuar – lost their lives together with many important men. It was a great Saxon victory and considerably reduced Danish strength and power.

In the Saxon period Tettenhall was a Royal Manor and it included a portion of the Royal forest of Kinver (Kingsley/Tettenhall Wood). It became two manors, one owned by the King, Tettenhall Regis, and one owned by the collegiate church, Tettenhall Clericorum. Royal Free Chapels owed their allegiance to the King, not the bishop. There were several in this frontier district.

From the eighteenth century Tettenhall became a place for the well-to-do. They built their mansions up on the ridge where the air was pure and where they could survey their industrial kingdoms in the smoke-filled skies over neighbouring Wolverhampton.

By the mid nineteenth century the village, its two greens, hotels and inns provided a summer weekend playground for Wolverhampton's artisan classes. Lines taken from the Reverend Ferneyhough's poem of 1789 aptly portray the scene.

> *Here Hampton's sons in vacant Hours repair,*
> *Taste rural Joys, and breathe a purer Air.'* *(3)*

As an urban district, Tettenhall had its own identity, but it had to keep a wary eye on its larger and expansionist neighbour. Eustace Lees in his satirical poem The Smestow *(4)* makes much of the river as the line of defence, in protecting Tettenhall's green and pleasant land:

> 'This Colonel Fowler Butler
> A boat of coal to Newbridge drew
> And orders gave to scuttle her
> And other boats upended were
> From Walkers' wharf and Weavers
> And so they slowly built a dam
> And formed a sea.'

> 'At night a fog or mist at times
> We seem from sleep to waken
> But know that here the spirit broods
> Of Smestow still unshaken.'

Tettenhall was to stave off takeover until 1966, but in the end Lees' fatalistic lines proved true:

'But Wolves are Wolves where ere they be
And nature little alters.'

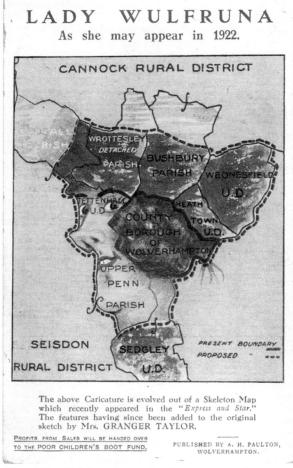

LADY WULFRUNA
As she may appear in 1922.

CANNOCK RURAL DISTRICT

WROTTESLEY DETACHED PARISH

BUSHBURY PARISH

WEDNESFIELD U.D.

TETTENHALL U.D.

HEATH TOWN U.D.

COUNTY BOROUGH OF WOLVERHAMPTON

UPPER PENN PARISH

SEISDON RURAL DISTRICT

SEDGLEY U.D.

PRESENT BOUNDARY
PROPOSED "

The above Caricature is evolved out of a Skeleton Map which recently appeared in the *"Express and Star."* The features having since been added to the original sketch by Mrs. GRANGER TAYLOR.

PROFITS FROM SALES WILL BE HANDED OVER TO THE POOR CHILDREN'S BOOT FUND.

PUBLISHED BY A. H. PAULTON, WOLVERHAMPTON.

Fig. 15   Wolverhampton's proposed
expansion, 1922

A postcard was produced in 1922 to show Wolverhampton's probable intention. The shape of Lady Wulfruna's head and hat was shown to cover not only the town, but the districts of Heath Town, Wednesfield, Bushbury, Wrottesley detached, Tettenhall, Upper Penn and Sedgley (5).

Up on the plateau is the site of Tettenhall Waterworks. The Wolverhampton Waterworks Co. was formed in 1844 and took powers in 1845 to sink wells into the Bunter Beds of the New Red Sandstone (Trias). It was the first attempt to supply Wolverhampton with clean water. Taken over by the Wolverhampton New Waterworks Company in the 1850s, additional plant, deeper wells and a reservoir were built at Tettenhall. Originally the potential yield from Tettenhall was 1.2 million gallons daily, but this had fallen to 800,000 gallons by 1968. Cosford Waterworks was opened in 1858 and water from the River Worfe and its boreholes was piped to Tettenhall. This extended the number of households that could be served in Wolverhampton (6). Tettenhall pump house is a listed building, whilst the reservoir has given way to housing. Regis Road was once called Waterworks Lane.

The district known as Newbridge at the foot of the scarp reminds us that this was the crossing point of the valley for those travelling to and from Shrewsbury, Chester and North Wales. Before the canal was built the water flow was more substantial and early on there was a need for a bridge. There appears to have been a new bridge as early as the twelfth century (7) and there was certainly one there by 1327, when Stephen at the new bridge was included in a list of tax payers for the Scottish war (8). The bridge in Meadow View carrying the old road over the Smestow was there by 1517 (9). A rebuilt County stone bridge, costing £4, is mentioned in 1710 (10). The building of Telford's A5 road to Holyhead and Ireland demanded another new bridge. Telford advised Francis Holyoake, Chairman of the Wolverhampton Turnpike Trust, to direct the road towards Aldersley and away from Old Hill, with its impossible gradient. The Trust did not take his advice. Neither did they comply when he suggested a short rising tunnel. Instead they built their line through the 'Rock'. The vast amount of spoil, thus created, was used to build a ramp. This carries the road over the Smestow and well above Lower Green, which gives a clue to the original road level. This new bridge dates from between 1820-3. It was only achieved with considerable difficulty and caused the bankruptcy of the first contractor as he had trouble in securing the foundations in the glacial sands and gravels of the valley floor. Tettenhall Urban District Council's first minute book of 1887 records the bridge abutments as in need of repair. By 1896 the Council's surveyor described the bridge as dilapidated *(11)*. *As already* mentioned, in 1933 a new culvert was constructed to carry the Smestow under the A41. The new bridge over the canal dates from 1939. We have a number of sketches reminding us of the Newbridge scene. Fullwood's sketch done in 1880 refers back to an earlier era and shows the old coach bridge over the Smestow, pre-1820 *(12)*. He notes that the limpid purity of the stream is no more and that pollution, the curse of the modern age, mingles with the current. Alan Wellings' drawing of 1929 depicts the three bridges at Newbridge, that over the canal, brook and railway. The Smestow bridge is that post-1820 *(13)*.

Fig. 16   Alan W. Wellings' 1929 illustration of the viaducts at Newbridge

The waters of the Smestow flow south and parallel to the ridge. Tettenhall College, a nonconformist foundation from the 1860s, still dominates the western heights. Set up to educate boys, it has moved with the times and has added girls to its complement. In 1944 it took over Tettenhall Towers, the adjacent property of the Thorneycrofts. Colonel Tom was a much respected village eccentric, an inventor, playwright and benefactor. He gave up iron making at the Shrubbery and Swan Garden Works in Wolverhampton, to act out the role of village squire. He died in 1903 as a result of an accident on the water chute at the Wolverhampton Industrial Exhibition of 1902. One of his sons, Colonel Alexander, was the hero of Spion Kop in the Boer War.

The Nuffield Hospital also has a prime position on the ridge. It lies on the site of Glen Bank, one of the Mander family (paint and varnish manufacturers) residences at Tettenhall.

There is still a significant girder bridge (warren truss bridge) in the valley. Known locally as the 'Meccano Bridge' it carries the railway walk over both Smestow and canal, as it moves from the west bank to the eastern flank on its journey south.

Before Compton is reached the Smestow is joined by the Graiseley Brook, which rises on Graiseley Hill and flows by way of Merridale, the Grammar School playing fields and Compton Park, where it fed the waters of a medieval moat. Its streambed once marked the boundary between Tettenhall and Wolverhampton. Before joining the Smestow

Fig. 17
Confluence of Graiseley and Smestow Brooks

it passes underneath the canal aqueduct, but it once joined slightly to the north of its present confluence.

It's at this point in the Smestow's journey that the mill leat, which fed Compton mill pond, left the main channel. Although the mill finished working about 1900, Edwardian postcards show the leat and ponds up against Henwood Road. Jones in his History of Tettenhall claims that the Smestow Mills were as old as the first

Fig. 18   Mill leat to Compton Mill

settlement and were certainly here by the Norman Conquest (14), but there is no mention of a mill in Domesday.

The mill was mentioned as one of two watermills of the King's Manor in 1249 (15). In 1326 John, son of William of Compton was licensed to grant Roger, son of Nicholas of Trescott, property which he held in chief in Compton. This included a mill. The lands, mill and mill house were said to be worth annually only 6 shillings and 8 pence, because the mill was in a dilapidated state and because the land was 'sandy and weak' (16). Roger still held the mill in 1338, when a suit brought against him over the ownership by William de Northwode was dismissed (17).

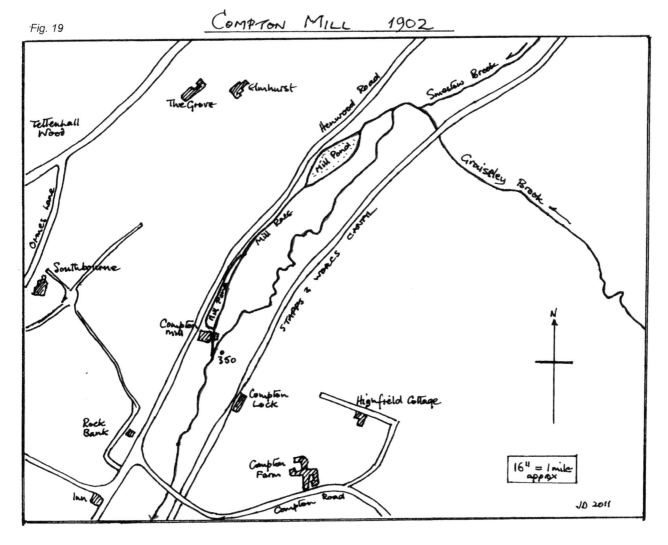

Fig. 19

21

In 1743 Compton Mill was described as a corn and blade mill *(18)*. The Victoria County History tells us that the copyhold of the mill was sold by Richard Cresswell, sometime before 1743, to John Shelton. The mill was later managed by the Allen family. For most of the nineteenth century it was a flour mill *(19)*. The buildings included a house and a two-storey mill, with an overshot wheel and two sets of stones.

The Bate family were machinists and millwrights here from at least the 1860s until the Second World War *(20)*. Enoch Wesley Bate took out a patent. His invention showed how two cast iron half couplings, bolted together around the wooden shaft, would hold firm and allow the mechanism to turn and rotate without falling apart, thus making for a smoothly operated mill *(21)*. By 1903, the mill lay disused *(22)*. The pool was drained in 1919 (site of the Boys Club and playing fields). Until the Second World War the lands on either side of the valley still had an agricultural use. In the last quarter of the nineteenth and the first quarter of the twentieth century the Wheelers farmed at Compton. Their lands ran down to the canal, but they were gone by the time that the railway opened, having sold off a great slice through their fields.

Fig. 20   Launch of the 'Compton Queen'

Just north of the village was Compton lock. This was the home of the Beech family who ran a fleet of rowing boats for hire, as well as their three steamers the 'Compton Queen', the 'Victoria' and the 'Margaret'.

In the village is Compton Hall, built in the first half of the nineteenth century for Thomas Elwell, a hardware merchant. A subsequent resident, Lawrence W Hodson – an admirer of William Morris – commissioned the wallpaper, which bears the village's name. It illustrates *'the final stage in Morris' development as a designer, in which he combined the naturalistic qualities of his early patterns with the more rigid designs he produced under the influence of his close study of the history of weaving'* *(23)*. Today, the house is the well known hospice.

The Smestow reaches congested Compton and flows underneath the Bridgnorth road. The ridges have closed in on both sides, giving meaning to the village name – 'the settlement in the narrow valley'. Here my forebears, the Willingtons carried on their trade as eighteenth-century lockmakers. Thomas Willington sold his wares wherever he could and certainly in Chester and Dublin. Chester was still a port for small ships at this time. His mail was left at

John Smith's turnpike at Newbridge *(24)*. In more recent time sandstone was quarried at Compton and sent by barge to Black Country foundries. It was also at Compton that the first sod was cut for the canal. From the lock there is a fall of 291 feet 8 inches to the River Severn at Stourport. The Smestow Brook and the industrial Stour must also make this journey. From Compton the canal continues to partner the brook on their descent, but here the railway parts company and leaves its sisters, before stopping at Compton Halt and cutting through the countryside on its way to Wombourne and beyond.

(1)   Express and Star Thursday May 16 1995, P13.

(2)   Notes and materials on The Battle of Tettenhall 910AD and other researches, David Horovitz. 2010.

(3)   Beautiful Village of Tettenhall, Reverend Ferneyhough, Newcastle 1810, P65.

(4)   The Smestow (TS), Eustace Lees, Whithead Bros, Wolverhampton 1929.

(5)   Lady Wulfruna as she may appear in 1922 - a postcard published by AM Paulton, Wolverhampton. Profits from the sale of the card go to the Poor Children's Boot Fund.

(6)   Wolverhampton Corporation Water Undertaking. Notes for Students 1964 and 1968.

(7)   A Tettenhall History, Geoffrey Hancock, Broadside 1991.P6.

(8)   Newbridge and its Bridges, Tettenhall Rock and the Holyhead Road (NBTRHR) Patrick Thom, The Staffordshire and Worcestershire Canal Society, 1988.

(9)   Victoria County History of Staffordshire (VCH) Volume XX, P13.

(10) Staffordshire Historical Collections (SHC), Volume 1934, P81.

(11) ibid NBTRHR.

(12) Remnants of Old Wolverhampton and Environs, John Fullwood, 1880.

(13) ibid TS Alan Wellings sketch.

(14) History of the Parish of Tettenhall, James P Jones, John Steen and Co, Wolverhampton, 1894.

(15) SHC Volume V (1), P180.

(16) SHC Volume 1911, P368-9.

(17) SHC Volume X1, P86

(18) VCH Volume XX, P34.

(19) ibid 17

(20) Various County Directories including Kelly's and William Whites Directory of Birmingham 1869.

(21) Enoch Wesley Bate Patent No 8436, 27th April 1895.

(22) OS Map 1/2500, 1902, Staffordshire 62:05

(23) The work of William Morris catalogue-an exhibition arranged by the William Morris Society at the Times Bookshop 1962, P73.

(24) The Willington Papers, A Dunphy, 1986

Fig. 21

GRAISELEY BROOK c. 1913 — much now culverted

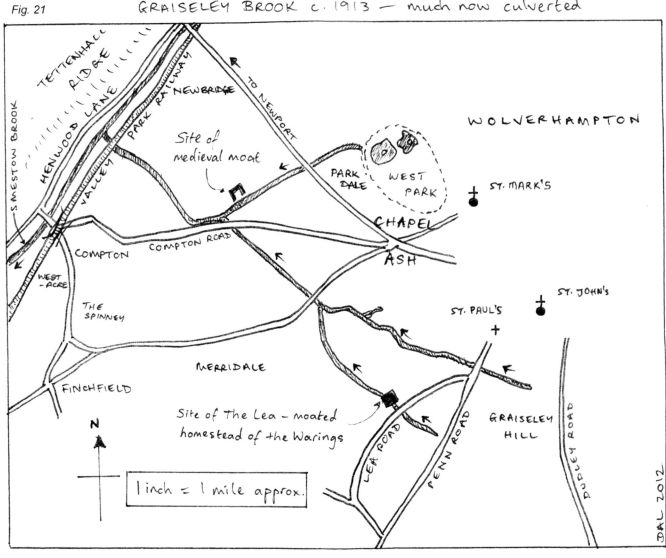

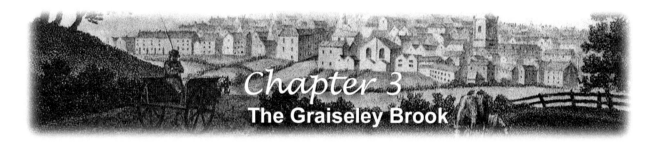

Chapter 3
The Graiseley Brook

The Graiseley Brook Tavern once stood at the junction of Penn Road and Sidney Street, a few hundred yards away from the site of St Paul's Church and today's ring road island. It was named after the watercourse which begins life on nearby Graiseley Hill and on the higher ground stretching back towards the Dudley Road.

A second source to the brook drained the ground upon which the Oaklands Road district was built. At the foot of the hill lay a medieval moated hall. It was called 'The Lea' and was the home of the Warings, a well-to-do family, which had gained its status from the wool trade. They became clothiers, Merchant Taylors and Citizens of London, but their roots lay in Lower Penn where they had been twelfth-century sub tenants. The name of Lea Road is well known to us. The Warings sold their estate in 1592 to William Baylie, gentleman, of Clements Inn for 200 marks of silver (£320). It consisted of house, two barns, 1 garden, 2 orchards, 10 acres of land, 6 acres of meadow and 50 acres of pasture, plus 2 acres of water (1). The hall was in a dilapidated condition by 1790, and it had gone by the late 1870s, to be replaced by Dalton Street. Today there is no surface evidence of a brook, it being part of the extensive road drain system, which feeds the Graiseley Brook at the bottom of the cemetery.

Long before our time the district was still rural with livestock grazing in the Penn fields. They would quench their thirst in the brook. As late as 1834 Frederick Calvert in his Picturesque Views of Staffordshire published an idyllic, if somewhat optimistic rural scene, as seen from the Penn Road and Graiseley Hill (2). Steen and Blackett published their guide to the town, with map, in 1871 (3). They show the Graiseley Brook still flowing through the fields, from besides Mander Street all the way across Merridale to the Compton Road and beyond. As if to stress

Fig. 22   View from Graiseley Hill across Penn Fields

the point, their guide was published to coincide with the visit of the Royal Agricultural show to Broadmeadow, the then racecourse and now the West Park. Factories and industrial housing had covered the area by the late nineteenth century.

Mr Beards of Pennfields *(4)* remembers the district as it was in 1937, when he travelled from Coalway Road, on the number 32 trolley bus, to school at Graiseley. The fare was just a halfpenny. Even then there was still the evidence of how pleasant this town fringe had been, as several of the large houses of nineteenth-century industrialists remained along the Penn Road. They could be found on both sides of Graiseley Hill. Several had their own woodland walks, with a pond or two in the grounds. These could be espied from the bus's top deck.

In those days the metal-bashing trades were still in the ascendancy, their factories covering much of the land between Brickiln Street, Penn and Dudley Roads and stretching further afield to Blakenhall. Tinplate, enamelling and galvanising were very much in evidence, but the district is world famous for its motor cycle and motor car production. Names such as AJS, Stevens, Diamond, Villiers, Star, Wolf, Clyno and Sunbeam were synonymous with the first thirty years of the twentieth century's developing form of transport. Indeed, Major Seagrave had set the world land speed record in March 1927 at Daytona Beach in Florida. He was clocked at 203.841 miles per hour in his 1000 horse power Sunbeam *(5)*. Workers at the factory nicknamed it the 'Slug'.

Mr Beards says that the brook crossed under Zoar Street in a culvert. This was in the sharp dip in the road before its junction with Merridale Street. He remembers it as an open brook in the recreation ground at the bottom of Fisher Street and says that the next time he had sight of it was in the allotments (where the Merridale flats are now). Additional water came out of a pipe at the bottom of the Jeffcock Road cemetery *(6)*. The Cemetery Company had been authorised by Act of Parliament in 1847, with the first internment taking place in 1850. The grounds had been laid out by a Penn man, Henry Beckett.

In 1937 the allotments could be seen from the footpath (now Aspen Way) from Oak Street and the area was known as 'The Slangs', a term which again refers back to the area's rural past. It was a very fitting use of the term for the allotments, as it means thin strips of land between the fields. The Beards family's coal merchant was a Mr Henry Wilkes. He lived in Owen Road and his yard was in the cul-de-sac end of Merridale Street. He always referred to the cemetery as 'Bromley's Orchard', the name doubtless remembering a former owner and land use *(7)*.

The brook crosses underneath Merridale Road in a culvert and flows alongside Gamesfield Green and the Grammar School, before passing under the Compton road.

The Graiseley Brook next appears in Compton Park, where it is joined by the water from the West Park Lake, which is released via a sluice and which is culverted towards Parkdale, Tettenhall Road and Paget Road. Much of the rainwater falling on the hill of Hampton would naturally end up in the West Park and Whitemore Reans areas. One such rivulet, the Puddle Brook, ran from the Horsefair (Civic Centre site).

The waters of the brook from the West Park once passed close by the moat of a medieval homestead in the fields of what became Chapel Ash Farm. One of the fields was called Moat Leasow.

The Graiseley Brook flows south of St Edmunds RC High School and heads for the Valley Park. It passes under both the former trackbed of the GWR's Wombourne line (south of the Meccano Bridge) and the canal. Its confluence with the Smestow was altered at the time of the building of the Staffs and Worcestershire Navigation and today it enters the Smestow a few hundred yards nearer to Compton *(8)*.

(1) The Wolverhampton Antiquary Volume 1. Gerald P Mander, P210, 377-388.

*(2) Picturesque Views and Descriptions of cities, towns, castles and other objects - Staffordshire.
Frederick Calvert, 1834, between P16-17.*

*(3) Steen and Blackett's Wolverhampton guide and Map. 1871. Sold by WH Smith and Son at the
town's railway stations and from booksellers*

(4) Mr Beards, Pennfields.

(5) Wolverhampton Red Book 1929, P230.

(6) ibid (4).

(7) ibid (4).

(8) Towpath Guide to the Staffordshire and Worcestershire Canal. J Langford, P105.

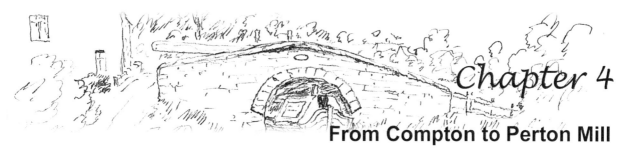

The river's name has been spelt in a variety of ways: Smethestall in 1300, Smestall on Saxton's map of 1577 and The Smestal in 1844 *(1)*. There are various explanations as to the meaning of the present name. Smestow in Old English is claimed to mean a small pool in a stretch of the river, a place for catching fish, where the water is still. It is also suggested that the word was first applied to one arm of the river before being transferred to its main course *(2)*. One expert goes back to the name Smethestall and says that it was made up of two parts: the one, 'staed', meaning a stagnant pool or place for catching fish; the other part, 'smelte', which means smooth water *(3)*. Duignan says that it is Middle English and means the stalls or places where smiths worked *(4)*. This may well be the case, for the river supported an early iron industry using charcoal supplies from Kinver Forest. Whatever the derivation Smestow is an old name, which replaced the earlier Celtic name of Tresel, which gave a physical description of the brook's waters.

Compton lock marks the summit of the Staffordshire and Worcestershire Canal Navigation. From here it drops through 291 feet 8 inches to reach the River Severn at Stourport, and the Smestow/Stour must do the same, even if by a different route. Compton is thought to be the first lock constructed by James Brindley on his Staffs and Worcs Canal and it can therefore claim to be the template for the Midland narrow canals *(5)*. The canal was navigable to Compton from Stourport late in 1770, eighteen months before it was open throughout. Compton was a busy transhipment centre for goods to and from Wolverhampton. The 1766 Act empowering the building of the cut only allowed the canal company to extract sufficient water for its operation. Surplus supply had to be returned to the brook through a series of weirs, which had a slightly lower sill *(6)*. An example lies south of Compton. This hopefully ensured that the many mills and forges had sufficient water to maintain their operations.

Between Compton and Wightwick the Smestow is partnered on its journey by the canal. There is still evidence of the once extensive quarrying for moulding sand, although nature has achieved its usual trick of healing most of the scars. The wharves along the Tettenhall Gap give us the evidence of this trade with the Black Country, which lasted up to the Second World War. A winding hole is located near to Wightwick Mill lock. It was used for turning the sand boats so that they could return to the foundries. There were many sandpits along the east bank, much of which is now in the Valley Park and Nature Reserve.

Nearby is Wightwick Mill, and like that at Compton, it was mentioned in 1249 in a deed of the Royal Manor of Tettenhall. By 1300 the Wrottesleys had ownership of the mill, but for a time there was much rivalry with the Perton family as both strived for domination of the district. The rights to Wightwick Mill were contested by the Pertons, but by 1343 Sir Hugh Wrottesley's rights had been recognised. In more recent time John Grove of Rugby, son and heir of Edmund Grove of Birmingham, a tallow chandler, conveyed the copyhold of the mill to Richard Fryer of Wolverhampton. He died six years later and the copyhold passed to his nephew, Richard Fryer of the Wergs. The mill had two sets of stones. In 1888 the waters ceased to drive the mill as it was converted to steam power *(7)*. It remained a corn mill and was still working in 1903 *(8)*. The mill buildings remain as a residence. They were once part of the farm complex. Robert Reade of Hillcroft Farm, Lower Penn, remembers his father taking the family by pony and trap to visit their relatives, Ernie Chidlow and their Auntie Ethel (Collins), at Wightwick Mill Farm. They travelled over the fields to the Bhylls, before driving down through the sandpits (Smestow School site), where in the season the martins were at play. They crossed the accommodation bridge over the canal, before the farm was reached. They would partake of a farmhouse tea of rashers of ham (cut from the flitches which hung from the ceiling), bread and butter and a piece of cake (with the smile in the top), and all washed down with a bowl of tea, before returning home. This was in the late 1940s. The mill had ceased working a generation before *(9)*. There is no public right of access to the mill or farm, which are private residences.

Fig. 23

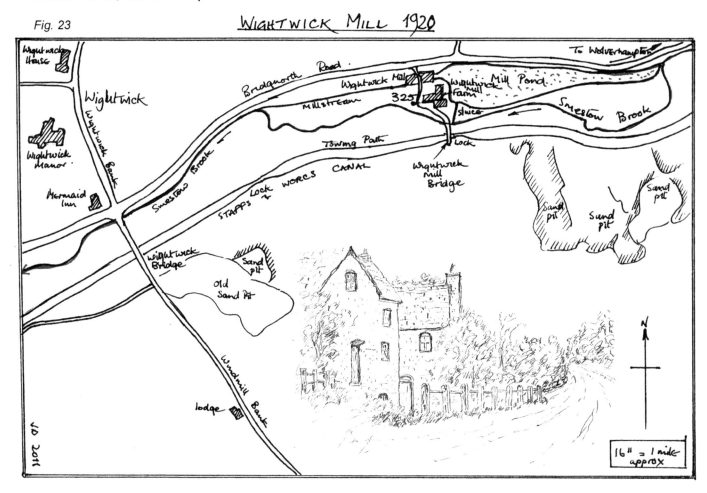

In 1972 heavy downpours in Wolverhampton caused the Smestow to overflow and enter the canal south of Compton. The canal returned the water by bursting its banks near to Wightwick Mill lock. In the process the towpath was swept away. Subsequently huge amounts of clay were required to fill the gap *(10)*.

At Wightwick Mill the Finchfield Brook is culverted under the canal before joining the Smestow. It has flowed by way of Goldthorn Hill, Bradmore and Finchfield, before passing under the Castlecroft Road and dropping down through the nature reserve.

The Smestow and the canal reach Wightwick and are crossed by the road bridge to Windmill Bank. On the west side is the old lime, sand and coal wharf. Across the Bridgnorth Road lies the Mermaid Inn and beyond, Wightwick Manor. This National Trust house, built in the late nineteenth century by the paint and varnish manufacturer Theodore Mander, is famous for its Pre-Raphaelite wallpapers, paintings, metalwork and glass. A stream flowing off Perton Ridge at Netherton (the lower hamlet, as opposed to the upper hamlet at Perton) graces the gardens before entering the Smestow. Some would say that Perton means 'pear' town, which refers to the 'Tettenhall Dick' variety, which is still found in the district.

Brook and canal, which have been irretrievably linked, part company at the end of the Tettenhall gap, the Smestow to flow through a gently sloping valley and the canal to cut south through Castlecroft, Lower Penn and Wombourne. Before leaving Wightwick we must remind ourselves that the name means a dairy farm in the bend of the river. This is a fitting description of the landscape as we enter South Staffordshire with its rural aspect, although these days dairy herds are hard to come by.

A mill leat once left the main channel just beyond Netherton, on its journey to Perton Mill. It was joined by the water of a small brook which flows off the ridge from Perton Court. This was once the site of a medieval moat, which surrounded Perton Hall. Ranulf, Lord of Perton had a watermill on the Smestow in the mid 1190s *(11)*. In the medieval period there were constant squabbles where mills were concerned. One such disagreement was between Ralph de Perton and the Abbot of Coombe Abbey in Warwickshire, whose grange or farm was situated at Trescott. Ralph admitted withholding an adequate water supply for Trescott Mill *(12)*.

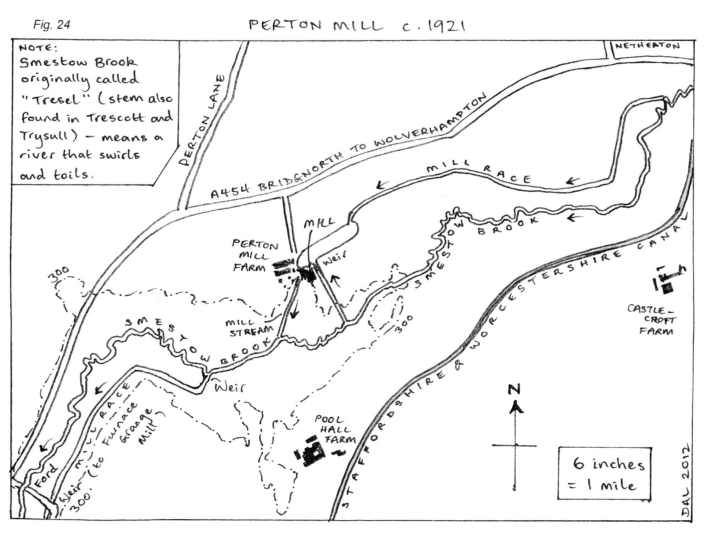

Fig. 24   PERTON MILL c.1921

NOTE:
Smestow Brook originally called "Tresel" (stem also found in Trescott and Trysull) – means a river that swirls and toils.

The mill buildings, which still remained in the 1970s were, apparently, built or repaired in 1766, a mill having stood on the site since at least the seventeenth century *(13)*. Both mill and header pond at Perton Mill Farm have gone, the last corn being ground in the 1920s. As farming in Britain continues to change and present challenges, this family farm of about 110 acres survives by hiring additional land for a few weeks/months and moving its flocks of sheep to available pasture.

Away to the north, beyond the ridge, is the mini town of Perton, built on the former Second World War airfield. This was opened in August of 1941 and after a brief spell under Army Co-operation Command it became a relief landing ground for a range of RAF stations. By 1943 it was a satellite of Wheaton Aston, fulfilling the role of an advanced flying training unit. It trained pilots on the twin engine Airspeed Oxford in flying, navigation, bombing, photography and blind approach training.

There was no night flying from Perton as the approach arc to runway number two included within it Courtaulds' factory chimneys, which were unlit for obvious reasons. Perton had no flare path, but night flying was practised during daylight hours by means of sodium lamps placed along the runway and with pilots wearing special goggles, which simulated darkness. On such occasions the plane taxied up the runway, the pilot flashed his identity letter at the tower and received a blinding green flash back on the aldis. The plane was off onto the 1400 foot runway. Engines revved, the plane shook and speeds of seventy to eighty miles an hour were reached, as the pilot eased the 'stick' back. The plane was airborne on its so-called 'night' flying exercise.

Pilots remembered Perton for the pronounced dip midway along its runway, which could be disconcerting for those flying in for the first time. There had been a First World War landing strip on the nearby fields. Perton was considered as a site for the town's airport in the 1930s. July 1947 saw the RAF's abandonment of the field. Today many of Perton's street names remind us of its former role *(14)*.

Also nearby along the plateau is Wrottesley Hall, or the rebuilt version of 1923, which replaced the larger building destroyed in the fire of 1897. The Wrottesleys can claim a presence from the twelfth century until the early 1960s, when they sold up their estate. From May of 1941 the parkland was home to the Princess Irene Brigade of the Royal Netherlands Army, named after Queen Wilhelmina's granddaughter. The Dutch Queen visited, as did Field Marshal Montgomery.

There was a third, but secret, military establishment on the ridge, housed in a hut to the north of Sling Wood from late 1940. This was a Y station, a high frequency intercept and direction finding radio monitoring unit. Codenamed 'Bert', it was part of MI8(a) & (b): Military Intelligence, Section 8, the signals intelligence group. It fed information to Beaumanor Hall in Leicestershire, itself linked to Station X, Bletchley Park *(15)*.

Below Perton Mill Farm is Trescott sewage outfall works of the Severn-Trent Water Authority. The brook winds its way through the countryside, being fished by heron, with mallard, coot, moorhen and dabchick in evidence.

(1) *Staffordshire Encyclopaedia. T Cockin. P522/3*

(2) *Staffordshire Place Names Part 1. JP Oakden. English Place Name Society. 1984 P18*

(3) *Staffordshire Place Names including the Black Country. Anthony Poulton Smith. 1995*

(4) *Staffordshire Place Names. WH Duignan. Henry Frowde. London. 1902. P139*

(5) *A Towpath Guide to the Staffordshire and Worcestershire Canal. J Ian Langford. Goose and son. P110*

(6) *ibid (5) P107.*

(7) *Victoria County History (VCH) Volume XX. P34*

(8) *Alan Godfrey Old Ordnance Survey Maps. Finchfield and Wightwick Sheet 62:09*

(9) *A Day Out with Robert Reade. Penn Parish Magazine December 2007. Angus Dunphy*

(10) *ibid 5*

(11) *Staffordshire Historical Collections Volume 111 (1). P222-3*

(12) *Penn to Paper. Angus Dunphy. P9-10*

(13) *Ibid (7).*

(14) *The Blackcountryman Volume 40 No. 3. The airmen of Perton. Angus Dunphy. P75-6*

(15) *Parish of Penn Magazine Feb 2012. The 'Y' Station on Perton Ridge. Angus Dunphy, P8-9. Support of Stephen King of Whitmore Reans is acknowledged.*

Fig. 25

FINCHFIELD BROOK c.1930

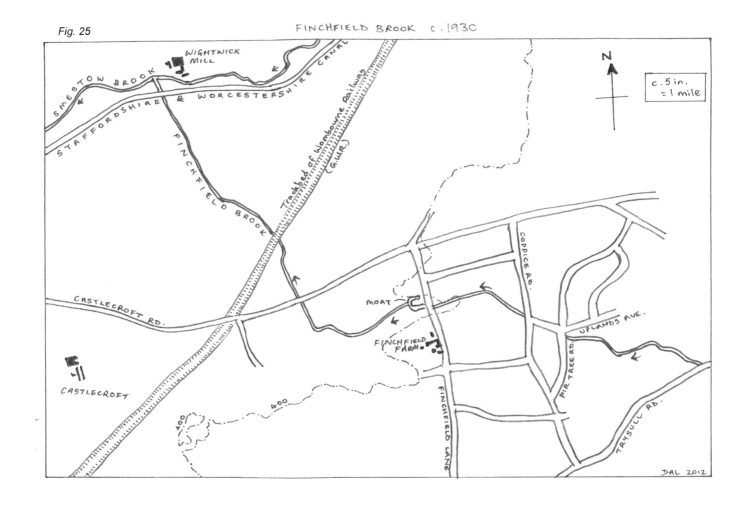

Chapter 5
The Finchfield Brook

The Finchfield Brook rises on the slopes of Goldthorn Hill, its highpoint being over 600 feet above sea level. Today the run-off is taken by the road drains. The rivulet reappears to the north of the Trysull Road before running parallel with part of Uplands Avenue and crossing Fir Tree Road and Coppice Lane (Road).

Much of this area was developed between the wars. William Hutchinson, at various times, owned Finchfield House, Ashleigh and Uplands and Finchfield Farms. He set about realising his assets. In the 1920s plots of land were sold off from the Broad Lane estate. Superior detached houses cost £800 and £1500 and bought a pair of upmarket semis. The company, called The New Lowland Estate Limited, subsequently owned Uplands Farm. It succeeded in gaining planning permission in 1933, to drain the land by laying a sewer along the valley of the Finchfield Brook, between Broad Lane, Uplands Farm and Finchfield Farm. Uplands Farmhouse was allowed to fall into disrepair. By 1935 the farm had shrunk to 14 acres and tenant Mr G Watkins was given notice to quit (1). The area between Broad Lane and Coppice Road was about to be developed, whilst much of the land from Coppice Road to Finchfield Lane would await post-war development.

The outbuildings at Finchfield Farm were tastefully turned into dwellings by Maythorn Construction in 1984. However, within a very few years the farmhouse itself and the flood meadow below it succumbed to further development. The farmhouse site, at about 400 feet above sea level, stands on a bluff above the valley of the Finchfield Brook. It was probably a successor to the homestead moat built in the valley below, sometime between the twelfth and fifteenth centuries. Three arms of the brook circled the homestead and offered defence (approximately seven feet depth), a barrier against wild animals and a ready food supply, as well as acting as a firebreak in what was a forested area. However, the raison d'être

Fig. 26   Barn conversion, Finchfield Farm

for the homestead may simply have been to make a statement about the social prestige of its owners.

The brook skirts Castlecroft Gardens before passing underneath Castlecroft Road and the trackbed of the Valley Park Railway Walk. Flowing in a north-westerly direction the brook drops down the bank of the park, alongside the old sandpits, to the canal at Wightwick Mill. It is about 330 feet above sea level.

Whilst the brook is insignificant in terms of volume, its waters were still precious to those operating the many mills and forges along the Smestow. At Wightwick Mill the Finchfield Brook passes underneath the canal to join the Smestow.

(1) Documents Wolverhampton Archives.

After Perton Mill a long leat, phlegm, flegm, fleam, or millrace left the river and flowed along the 300 foot contour towards Trescott Ford. In the 1930s and 1940s the smell from its sluggish waters was a constant cause of complaint from the villagers. It was culverted underneath the bend on Ford Lane, where there was a weir to return excess water back to the brook. The phlegm flowed through the sheep meadows to below Trescott Grange Farmhouse, where it was crossed by a cart bridge. It continued across Phlegm Meadow to nearby Furnace Grange, where it fed the mill, before the mill stream returned its water to the river.

Trescott Ford is notorious for catching motorists, who believe their vehicle can ride the waves, when the Smestow is in full spate. They ignore the depth gauge at their peril.

However, the ford is a local feature and long may it remain. In the dry summers of 1975 and 1976 when hosepipe bans were in force, it was used by the inventive as a car wash. I have also seen workers washing in it after a hot day picking peas.

Fig. 27   The Smestow at Trescott Ford

The Smestow's waters flow westwards, with the farming hamlet well above the river valley. Whilst the dependency on the land has gone for all but a few, attractive properties such as East and West Trescott Farmhouses and the Thatched Cottage remain to remind us of the recent past. The footpath from Trescott Grange to the Bridgnorth Road, which crosses over the Smestow by a footbridge, is an attractive walk at any time of year. (Lower Penn path 7, Wrottesley/Perton path 18).

Trescott Grange lies above the flood plain on the south bank and was an early homestead site, which prospered but in our time has receded in importance. There are two unconnected early charters which refer to Trescott. The first notes that in 985 King Ethelred granted one manse at Trescott to Lady Wulfruna. She gave it to the church at Wolverhampton (Wulfruna's High Town). The second refers to the 1190s and is important because during that period William Buffary, Lord of Lower Penn, granted the land around Trescott to the monks of Combe Abbey, in Warwickshire. They set up their grange, or farm, here. Dr Peter King makes a strong case as to the location of the land (1). He suggests that the lands were on the Lower Penn side of the brook, along the northern boundary and western extremity of the parish. They can be identified on the nineteenth century tythe map of Penn as a much older landholding by their irregular field boundaries and as a large property belonging to the Wrottesleys. They included the lands of Trescott and Furnace Granges as well as of Pool Hall. This fits with the acquisition of part of the Lordship of Trescott from William Wollaston by Sir Walter Wrottesley, the second baronet, 1659-86. Trescott hamlet on the other side of the brook lay in the ancient parish of Tettenhall. At

Furnace Grange the Smestow turns south; the lands to the east of the canal show straightforward and regular hedge lines and reflect strips and parcels of land.

It was usual for a medieval noteworthy to give lands to the church in perpetuity, so that the monks could pray for his soul. Such gifts, however, were less welcome to the donor's relatives as they found their rents curtailed. This was in fact the case with William's widow, Sibelle, who on 8th July 1200 petitioned that some of the Trescott lands belonged to her. Abbot William Fitz Wido, not wishing to disinherit a widow, promised her twenty shillings and eight pence yearly, but the lands remained the property of the church *(2)*.

The monks established fishponds and dovecotes to supply their needs. They also built a mill, which would not only grind their corn, but provide revenue from other users. Many were the disputes over mills and their supply of water. In a previous chapter there was an example of how Ralph de Perton withheld a sufficient supply of water from Trescott Mill *(3)*, which probably lay at Furnace Grange.

Almost one hundred years later the medieval mind seems to have altered little. In 1272 Roger Buffary sued Philip, Abbot of Combe, for a messuage and six virgates of land and a mill at Trescott. The Abbot defended his right and the case was adjourned to Salop *(4)*. Members of monastic orders and their workers were also often miscreants. A year earlier, in 1272, Brother John Burel, with others, stood accused of stealing the King's venison from Kinver Forest. It is to be remembered that a royal forest was for the King's pleasure and that the deer were his. A 'forest' was an area of land, not necessarily all woodland, and in this instance it extended to Wombourne, Orton and Lower Penn, the Smestow being its northern boundary, except for the wood of Kingsley (Tettenhall Wood).

The medieval period and the privileged position of the church came to an end with the Tudor monarchs. It was Henry VIII who swept away the monasteries in the years 1536-40. After this time Trescott Grange's ownership was in the hands of gentlemen. The Wollastons acquired the property in 1557 and retained it through much of the Stuart period – the parish registers give us much information. After William Wollaston (died 1604) came Hugh who was buried in 1610. Edward (died 3rd January 1630) was next in line, but as he was then a minor the property was let to Walter Leveson of Wolverhampton *(5)*.

The house was next occupied by Hervey Bagot, later to be created a baronet. He was at the Grange until about 1623. Three of his six children were born here, Edward, Hervey, and Richard (1616/17/18). As children they would have played in the water meadows and fished in the brook, but they were to play far more difficult roles in the Civil War in this locality. Hervey the third son was actively engaged in the service of the King up to the date of the surrender of the Close at Lichfield in 1646. At this time he was second in command of the garrison and held the rank of colonel.

Richard, the fourth son, had as godfathers two near neighbours – Edward Sutton, Lord Dudley, who was living at Himley and Walter Wrottesley of Wrottesley. Richard appears to have attracted the attention of Prince Rupert, by whom he was made Governor of Lichfield in 1643. It seems likely that he was a professional soldier, as was common with younger sons of noble families. He resigned his governorship and returned to fight with the forces in the field, where he had command of a regiment of horse. Injured at Naseby, he died of his wounds at Lichfield and lies at rest in the Cathedral *(6)*.

Edward, the second son, succeeded to the family title and was returned as Member of Parliament for the County in the first parliament of the reign of Charles II.

In the 1640s Trescott Grange was the home of Richard Chapman. In 1979, when St Bartholomew's Church at Penn was undergoing alterations his tablet was rediscovered below the chancel floor. The stone was broken and now rests under the High Altar, but Shaw, the Staffordshire historian writing in 1800, gives the inscription (7). He states that Richard was the first owner of the Grange, suggesting that the house was newly rebuilt. Richard was a wealthy man and a person of importance in seventeenth century Penn as his burial under the chancel in April 1645 shows. At one point during the Civil War he was paying £25 to the Parliamentary County Committee as they forced taxes out of the local people. His wealth and good standing is further shown in the parish register dated 5 November, 1644, where he is trusted to hold money – 20 shillings – for the parish to use with the poor. William, his son, is mentioned in the parish register as having been buried on 26 October, 1656.

In the late 1630s the stories of Trescott and Furnace Granges begin to diverge, the one keeping its farming role, the other becoming an industrial unit. Three members of the City of London's Fishmongers Guild – Peter Hassard, Henry Wollaston and Richard Wollaston – sold the iron furnace and three corn mills at Trescott, to Thomas Foley and William Normansell, his brother-in-law. Plainly, the Wollastons had kept their industrial interests alive in the parish until this time.

The Hearth Tax returns of 1666 give us the information that John Finch of Trescott Grange headed the Penn list with 12 chimneys. He was a competitor in the iron trade to the Foleys, but had come to a trade agreement with them, which left him running Grange Furnace and Greens, Swin and Heath forges. The parish registers refer to the men of standing who were living at Trescott Grange in this period – John and Elizabeth Muchall were in residence in August 1676, when their son Thomas was baptised; whilst a 1682 entry in the parish registers announces the burial of Elizabeth as well as referring to 'the newhouse at the Grange'. We therefore have another date for at least part of the house. However, we also know that John Finch had sold the Grange Farm to Sir Walter Wrottesley by 1686 (8).

Grange Furnace was at the forefront of the new technologies of the charcoal-based iron smelting industry. Iron making was evident in Kinver Forest from as early as the 1300s, based on the bloomery, where iron was heated using charcoal. This method only gave a small low-quality production. It was replaced in the 1630s by the new methods of the Stour Valley and its tributary the Smestow Brook. The technological breakthrough was the blast furnace, using water power to drive a large wheel, which compressed alternately two pairs of bellows. These blew an almost continuous flow of air through the tuyere, or blast pipe, and onto the furnace (9).

The charcoal fuel to heat the ore was supplied to Grange from an area of country that stretched from south of Bridgnorth northwards to Newport and Stafford. The iron ore was brought by packhorse and cart from the Wednesbury district and limestone from Dudley and Sedgley.

Grange Furnace would have been square in construction, made from fire-resistant natural rock. Dr King has suggested that the sandstone may well have come from Himley, as the lease of Cradley Furnace allowed Thomas Foley to take hearths from a quarry there. The Keuper Sandstone of the Orton Hills may also have been used in building the furnace. Bricks, made from marl dug in nearby fields, would also have been used. The hearth would have been two feet across, but as the furnace rose in height, so did the internal gap widen. At the opening a connecting ramp allowed labourers to tip barrow-loads of ore, charcoal and limestone into the furnace to keep it topped up. The hearth would have been tapped every twelve hours or so and the molten metal run off into channels in the receiving sand beds, known as sows and pigs – these patterns represented piglets suckling from their mother. The hot iron was thereafter known as pig.

Grange Furnace needs to be seen as an integral part of a complete cycle of iron production. Its relationship with the forges at Greene's (Greensforge), Heath (Heathmill) and Swin (Swindon) was that of supplier of 'pig'. The forge turned it into bar iron. This was further transhipped to a slitting mill such as the one at the Hyde, where rods were produced. So we have a picture of a well established seventeenth-century iron industry in the Smestow Valley, based upon water power and charcoal.

The interests of the industry are tied to the commercial skill of one family, the Foleys. Richard (1588-1657), a nailer, was responsible for mechanising the process of slitting bar iron. His third son, Thomas (1616-1677), continued the process of building their interests and Thomas' youngest son, Philip (1653-1716), assumed command of the Stour Valley iron interests. They were linked, through his brother Paul, to the Forest of Dean's iron trade. At one time Philip operated 21 separate establishments, which included four furnaces, 13 forges and 3 slitting mills. Philip's book of stock, which survives, gives much detail of the transactions between the various plants. Grange was valued at £2800 in 1669 and this was made up of outstanding debts and money given for materials, as well as for carriage. Thomas Hatton of Dalicott owed £8-19-4. £669-6-4 was in John Shawes' hands as money paid on account for *'wood cutting, cording and coling charcoles' (10)*.

By the early 1660s the Foleys had problems of access to their furnace, for the surrounding land was now owned by the Earl of Dorset. He had inherited the Lordship of Trescott from his kinsman, Sir Richard Leveson *(11)*. The Earl attempted to extract £500 per annum for passage over his land. The Foleys answer was for the Earl to buy the furnace for £600, together with a pair of corn mills, worth £12 per annum. Presumably they won their argument, but whether they continued to pay as little as four shillings and four pence a year is not known. Did they cease production for a time? Eventually Sir Walter Wrottesley purchased the Lordship of Trescott from the Earl of Dorset.

It's almost by accident that we know who was living in Grange Mill house in 1677. The following year James Illingworth wrote his account of the man whose *'legs rotted off'*. John Duncalf had led a dissolute life and had been given a prison term for stealing his master's iron, but was released claiming to be sick. He continued in his old ways and stole a bible from Humphrey Babb's Grange Mill house. He asked his wife, Margaret for some food and small drink and as she knew him she agreed. Whilst she was getting this he stole her bible. He then sold it to one of John Downing's maids at Heath Forge in Wombourne for three shillings. He returned to Kingswinford and the story of his actions eventually became public knowledge. He denied the accusation and said that if he was lying then God would let his legs drop off. They did and he repented before he died *(12)*.

Grange was not always in blast (e.g. it stood in 1664, 1669, 1672) as production always depended upon demand for pig iron. It would have produced some 400 tons per year between 1692 and 1697. In 1668 it produced 605 tons. Its 'pig' was of coldshort quality, which went amongst other uses for the manufacture of forge hammers and heavy anvils *(13)*. Dr Peter King's researches show that Philip Foley sold the site for £400 in 1708 for conversion to a corn mill, with an extra £400 to be paid if it was used as an ironworks *(14)*. Grange was certainly in blast in the period 1728/9, so market forces and the price of iron had ensured its continuance. The parish registers refer to Grange throughout the period, as its workers are baptised, married and buried. William Phillips had died there in 1638; Thomas Smyth in 1666; Old Bob, probably a labourer, in June 1666; whilst James Wirsedale, son of Francis and Mary, was baptised there in May 1718. Other baptisms followed – on 6 April 1724, Hannah, daughter of John and Ann Hawkins; on 7 July 1726, John, son of William and Mary Carter; on 15 November 1734, Joseph, son of Robert and Esther Rostance. William Shenton was the first eighteenth-century occupier of Grange to be mentioned. His burial is noted in the parish register as on 21st November, 1728. He is *'as of Grange Hall'. (15)*.

One family dominates the later years of iron-working. The Jordans were operating Grange Furnace and nearby Heath Forge, by the 1740s. The family gravestone lies behind the chancel at St Bartholomew's Church in Penn. It tells us that *'William Jordan of Grange Furnace died in his 84th year in the year of our Lord, 1752, and his wife Susannah in 1759'*. Their offspring Thomas and his wife Mary began raising their family at Grange Furnace, rather than at Furnace Grange, showing that industrial rather than farming interests were still uppermost. Indeed, 1772 saw the completion of the nearby Staffordshire and Worcestershire Canal Navigation, with its dock at Dimmingsdale. It is almost certain that this was built to transport goods for the furnace *(16)*. However, the development of the Black Country coalfield and the new coking technologies heralded the end for Lower Penn's iron industry. Of Thomas and Mary's 12 children (born between 1773 and 1796,) the youngest child, William Stubbs Jordan, turned to farming at Furnace Grange *(17)*. He was still there at his death in 1870. His brother Edward's service in the Peninsular War against Napoleon makes interesting reading and is told elsewhere *(18)*.

The Wrottesleys sold Furnace Grange Farm in 1950, and the farms of Trescott Grange and Pool Hall in 1963. The Wrottesleys held sway in these parts until that final sale of their estates in 1963.

In the nineteenth century Lower Penn and particularly this western corner of the parish were engaged in farming. Over time farming tenants came and went with the quarter days and one such advert in the Wolverhampton Chronicle of March 1854 illustrates this:

'Household furniture, dairy and brewing utensils, ale and beer casks, fixtures and a variety of useful effects belonging to Mr Henry Harris. Upon the premises - 13 well seasoned feather beds, 44 pairs of sheets, 20 pairs of blankets, oak and mahogany chests, grand pianoforte, china etc'

Of the mills at Furnace Grange, by the 1860s there was but one, operated by John and then Joseph Miller, farmers and millers here until the mid 1890s. Subsequently they set up a steam-operated corn mill in Wolverhampton on Corn Hill. By this time the use of the Smestow's power was in sharp decline. Furnace Grange Mill continued working until the 1920s, with only the larger mills able to struggle on for a few more decades. The mill building, with a tablet inside commemorating the Millers, survives and is today used as a store shed.

After Furnace Grange the Smestow turns south as it heads for Seisdon.

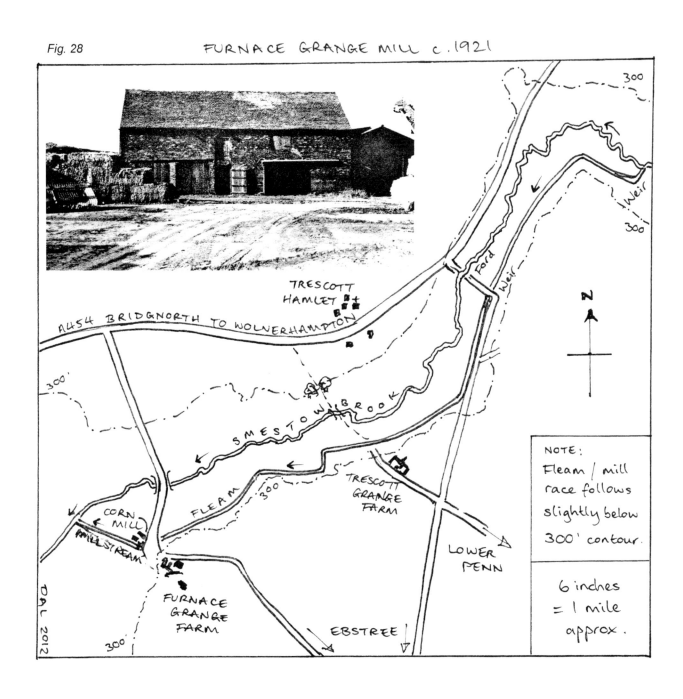

Fig. 28   FURNACE GRANGE MILL c.1921

(1)   Correspondence with Dr King.
(2)   Penn to Paper. A Dunphy. 1996. P9-15 and Staffordshire Historical
        Collections (SHC) Vol 3, 1882. P170, 221, 222.
(3)   SHC Vol 3, P222.
(4)   SHC Vol IV, 1883. P206. Investigating Penn, Editor TR Bennett, WEA
        Wolverhampton, P26-7.
(5)   Penn Parish Register Vol 1. Staffordshire Parish Register Society 1921. A
        History of the Family of Bagot. Maj-General The Hon Geo Wrottesley. SH
        Collections Vol XI New Series, 1908. P102-5
(6)   ibid Penn Parish registers.
(7)   The History and Antiquities of Staffordshire Vol 2. S Shaw. P218
(8)   History of Wrottesley. SHC Vol VI New Series Part 11, 1903. P336-7
(9)   Penn in Print. A Dunphy. 2000. P87-90
(10) A Selection from the Records of Philip Foley's Stour Valley Iron works 1668-
        74. RG Schafer. Worcestershire Historical Society New series Vol 9, 13
(11) Investigating Penn. Ed. TR Bennett. WEA, Wolverhampton. P31-2
(12) A Just Narrative or Account of the Man whose hands and legs rotted off in
        the Parish of Kingswinford in Stafford-shire, where he died June 21 1677.
        Carefully collected by Jam. Illingworth, B.D. An eye and ear witnefs of
        moft of the material paffages in it. London. Printed by Hen Browne at the
        Gun at the weft end of St. Pauls, 1678.
(13) ibid 10.
(14) The Blackcountryman Vol 41 No 3. Dr Peter King P50. The complete article
        is recommended for a detailed study of Grange.
(15) ibid parish registers.
(16) A Towpath Guide to the Staffordshire and Worcestershire Canal. J Ian
        Langford. Goose, 1974. P114
(17) Out and About in Penn. A Dunphy. 1990. P30-33
(18) Penn and Ink. A Dunphy. 1992. P15-18

Fig. 29

THE BLACK & NURTON BROOKS

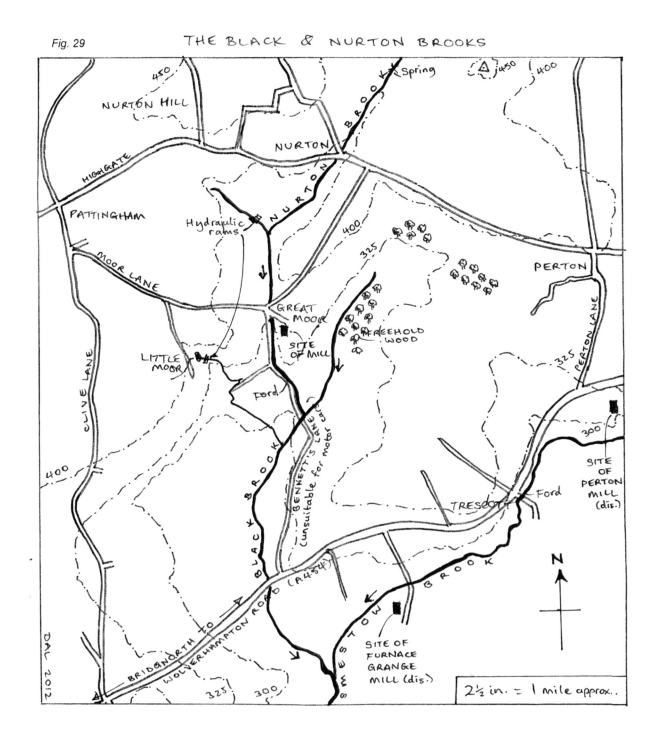

44

Both these brooks run off the Pattingham-Perton Ridge, and after joining in Bennett's Lane flow down to join the Smestow.

The Nurton Brook begins life in a number of springs, which lie on both sides of Nurton Hill. The eastern branch flows through Nurton hamlet and underneath the Pattingham Road. After passing two or three fields, it is joined by its western arm, the public footpath from New Buildings Farm to Great Moor crossing the confluence. Here, hydraulic rams were in place. These worked on the principle of using the force of water in a stream, through a self-acting pump, to push a smaller amount of water back up to a reservoir. The system was widely in use on many estates in the last quarter of the nineteenth century and up to the time of the Second World War. It allowed for a much wider access to water for the rural community and included irrigation of fields and the supply of water for stock. A further set of rams were located at Little Moor, before the rivulet ran down to join the Black Brook.

At Great Moor the Nurton Brook crosses underneath the road and runs into the Great Moor Farm complex. Here was an overshot wheel fed by a pool. The wheel supplied power for a range of farmyard machinery and was in use until the Second World War *(1)*. A photograph of it appeared in the Wolverhampton Journal of 1908 *(2)*. This site had supported a mill as far back as 1312. In that year Nicholas de Stirchley and Adam at the Gate of Trescote were accused of turning the water at 'Le More' outside of its course. Thomas in 'Mora' had a tenement here in 1314 *(3)*. Whilst the mill wheel has gone the tailrace is piped across a field to join the Nurton Brook in Bennett's Lane.

Fig. 30   Great Moor millwheel

This lane is a well-known local feature as the brook flows down it for a considerable distance, giving the car driver an extended ford to navigate. If children are on board they find the 'watersplash' a wonderful adventure, particularly if another vehicle is met in the lane!

Bennett's Lane was probably the scene of escaping robbers in 1992. Armed men held up two security men at the rear of the National Westminster Bank in Anders Square, Perton. They made the Group 4 men drive their van in convoy to an isolated field off Great Moor Road. Here they forced the third guard, in the sealed compartment, to pass out cash for fear of what could happen to his colleagues. The robbers drove off in a Protec van, which had been run by a Leicester-based security firm before they had gone into liquidation the previous year. It is thought the raiders left via Bennett's Lane and the 600 yard ford, before turning east along the

Bridgnorth Road and Trescott ford. Here, they proceeded to Dimmingsdale, Penstones and Blackpit Lane, where they changed into their getaway vehicle. The crime remains unsolved (4).

The Black Brook begins in the fields of South Perton Farm, famous as the Tettenhall Horse and Donkey Sanctuary and for the 'Strongest Man' competitions. It flows parallel to the ridge, before running alongside Freehold Wood. To the north a heron nests in Sling Wood. At the confluence with the Nurton Brook, the Black Brook keeps its name, the joint waters cutting across Bennett's Lane to flow on its western side. It is not long before the stream that began life at Little Moor adds its weight to the waters.

A little to the south the Black Brook passes close by the site of the former Tettenhall Urban District Council's sewage plant of 1890. Built at a cost of £14,000, its purpose was to alleviate the emptying of the district's waste into the Smestow at several points. The sewage was now collected at Compton, from both the Tettenhall and Finchfield sides of the valley, before it was piped to the Black Brook Valley Works (5).

The plant included reception tanks, a mixing house, three precipitation tanks and two storage tanks with connecting channels. There was also a manager's house. However, the works relied on land on which to tip out the sludge, so that it could dry. The location was a poor one, for the valley lies in a natural drainage basin, below the ridge, and thereby the soils are of a heavy peaty nature. For successful sewage irrigation free-draining soils are essential. The name of the adjacent wood, 'Rushy Marsh', should have been heeded by the planners. The problems were compounded by mixing surface water drainage with raw sewage. Tettenhall Council, like many others, had the notion that crops could be grown on the land, thus reducing the cost to the residents. It was to learn that there were better ways of processing sewage, which did not include farming large tracts of land. An alternative works was built in the 1930s, itself to be superseded by the Trescott Works on the Smestow in 1961. Today the Black Brook Valley Works is silent and the manager's house, much enlarged and improved, is a private residence.

The Black Brook flows underneath the Bridgnorth Road, its flow considerably reduced since the closure of the works. It passes by the garden centre and flows towards the barns called 'Little Burbrook', which lie in the fields to the south. Shortly afterwards the Black Brook joins the greater Smestow.

(1) Pattingham. Brighton. E. Blocksige, Dudley 1942. P160.
(2) Wolverhampton Journal 1908. P182.
(3) Pattingham Register. Staffordshire Parish register society 1934. Gerald Mander. PXIV.
(4) Penn in Print. Angus Dunphy. P85-6.
(5) The Industrial Archaeologist Magazine November 1966. N Mutton. P261-7.

Fig. 31

SEISDON MILL TO TRYSULL MILL

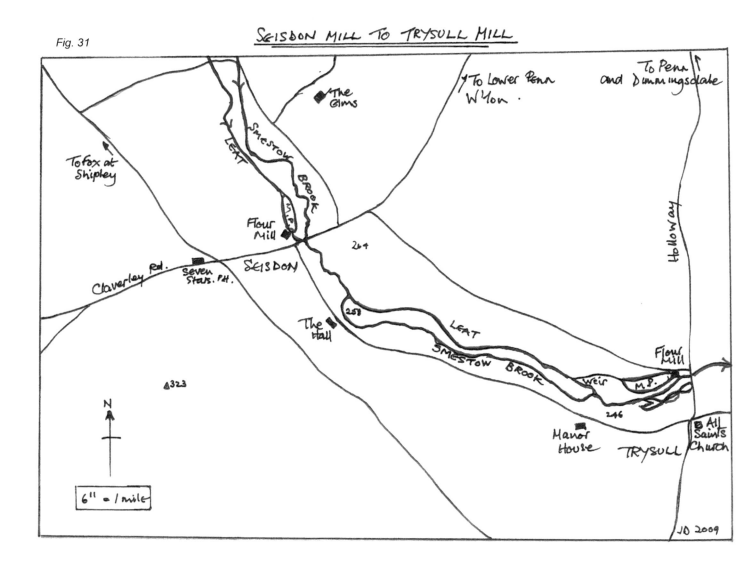

These important villages have given their names to either the hundred or to the rural deanery. In the case of the former the name means Saxon Hill and refers to the escarpment beyond Seisdon Common, known as Abbots Castle or Apewood Castle Hill. Evidence of hut circles and ditches can still be seen along the footpath which traverses the ridge. These belong to at least the Dark Age period. Here is also good evidence of the Roman occupation, for the road from Greensforge Camp and Droitwich passes beneath on its way to Uxacona, or Oakengates, on Watling Street. In 910 it is likely that Saxon watchers, positioned on the ridge, would have seen the Danes, laden with their booty, making their way from Quatford to Tettenhall by way of what was left of the Roman road.

A three-sided erratic, a granitic boulder, called 'The Warstone' was found at the lay-by on the B4176. It marked the spot where the lands of three Roman colonists met. It was the meeting point of the three parishes of Swindon (at one time Swindon was in Wombourne parish), Bobbington and Trysull & Seisdon (1). The boundary has been slightly altered in recent times.

Trysull derives its name from the Celtic word, Tresel, the former name of the Smestow. It is a chocolate-box village, with its ancient church, green and an assortment of Georgian and Victorian houses and farmsteads. Dr Johnson was brought to Trysull Manor, the home of distant relatives, in 1711 to be treated for an eye complaint by Dr Thomas Attwood (2).

On leaving Furnace Grange, at the extremity of Lower Penn parish the Smestow tumbles over one of several weirs on its journey to Trysull. These were placed in the stream's bed to maintain a head of water, whilst sometimes they were used on a millrace's bank to return excess flow to the main stream. Soon after the weir is the confluence with the Black Brook, which has drained the land below Perton Ridge, from The Clive and Great Moor to Nurton and Perton.

Alongside Wash House Lane, now called Alms House Lane, the fleam for Seisdon Mill left the river. Both flowed under Post Office Lane in their own channels. A sluice and cast iron winding gear allowed excess water to be returned to the river. At this point the footpath from Buckhouse to the mill hugs the former fleam bank. The Smestow flows a little way to the east and passes close by The Elms, renowned for its Summer Solstice Evening of music and village companionship. Through the generosity of its owners the considerable funds raised have gone to support Trysull Parish Church (3).

Near this spot is the Seisdon receiving station of Esso's Midline Pipeline. It has come from Fawley on Southampton Water and within it oil and petroleum products are pumped 130 miles to the Midlands. Built at a cost of £40 million, it was constructed in 1985 (4).

Another weir lay at the start of the mill pond, whilst a sluice fed the overshot wheel (5). Overshot wheels needed a good head of water to drive them, but were the most efficient as there was little water loss. The water fell from above the level of the wheel, into the buckets near its crest, and the weight brought the wheel into motion.

There was a mill at Seisdon by the thirteenth century, for an assize held at Stafford in 1227 (the very year that King Henry III came of age) dealt with a case brought by Walter de Bradelea (6). He claimed his father, Geoffrey, had held half the mill at his death. Simon de Tresel held the mill and the jury found that his father, Bernard, had held it for half a year before Geoffrey's death.

By the early seventeenth century Ambrose Grey was Lord of the Manor. He granted a lease, for the mill and other lands, to Thomas Dolman for the life of his three sons. There was to be an initial payment of £45 and then an annual rent of £3-13-10 (7).

Fig. 32   Seisdon Mill and Farm

The existing red-brick mill building is eighteenth-century and fits in architecturally with the adjacent mill house, which has a date stone of 1749. In its later years it is linked with the Wrottesley family who were Lords of the Manor. They leased it to the Bantons at The Old Manor House (the early part of the house has a date stone inscribed 1684), who were early nineteenth century agricultural improvers. Daniel Banton was the first in the county to use guano to fertilise his 300 or so acres. He put Seisdon Mill to a new use and by a series of connecting rods and timbers linked the mill apparatus to his threshing machines, in the barns across the road. This was done by building culverts under the road and until recent time the brass inspection covers could be seen. The threshing machines performed several operations at once, which included 'thrashing, winnowing, shaking the straw, piling the barley, bagging up the grain and weighing ready for market' (8). The mill also ground cattle feed.

The mill was sold by the Wrottesleys in 1929, but continued operating using electricity until after the Second World War.

Fig. 33 SEISDON MILL c. 1920

There was a bridge over the Smestow on Ebstree Rd. at Seisdon from about 1300. The route linked Wolverhampton with Claverely. In 1826 the present three-arched county bridge was built (9). Beyond Seisdon Hall another fleam broke away from the main river on its journey to feed the then mill pool at Trysull. The fleam lay north of the river's course.

This stretch of the river was known as the Trysull Brook (10). The valley was carved by escaping meltwater at the end of the last ice age, when the Tettenhall Gap was created and the sand and gravel beds were laid down at Seisdon and Trysull. These continue in a long esker type formation to Kingswinford and Wordsley. At Lowe's Trysull sandpits a mammoth's tooth was found in 1969, reminding us that these creatures roamed our countryside in inter-glacial periods. (11).

As the Smestow reaches Trysull it passes by a number of interesting houses, the foremost of which is Trysull Manor, its earliest parts dating back to at least Jacobean times, if not Elizabethan (12). It is well worth catching a glimpse of the welcoming message on its walls:

'Stranger should this catch your eye,
do a favour passing by,
Bless this house ere you be gone
And it shall bless your passing on' (13).

The village has always had a mill, for it was a necessity of settled life. One is mentioned at the time of Domesday in 1086, when it was worth four shillings, whilst the village amounted to thirty shillings value (14). The mill's successors are recorded in several medieval documents, when it was referred to as 'Heykeleye' (15), a term still used to denote the fields beyond 'Ovens End' and below the old workhouse. It means a river bank or terrace. In 1356 Richard in the Lone, of Wolverhampton, was brought before the court for taking ironwork from Trysull Mill, valued at 100 shillings. In his defence he claimed that Richard Evendon, who had brought the case against him, was his tenant and that he had not paid his annual amount of 13 shillings and four pence in lieu of fealty and service (16). The case was adjourned until witnesses could be called. In 1412 a case was brought against the notorious robbers known as John and William Myners and John Hardhead, who had led an insurrection against the King (17). In a planned attack on the mills around Wolverhampton, Dunstall, Dom (on the headwaters of the Penk), Gorsebrook, Seisdon and Herclyf (Trysull), much damage had been done and much property stolen. The purpose was to stop the villagers grinding corn and to stop the King's subjects sending food to the town, so that its inhabitants would perish. The amazing postscript to the events was that they were pardoned for all their felonies; they must have paid the King a heavy fine to escape their treachery. When Trysull Mill moved to its present site is unknown.

The mill is shown on Yates' map of the county dated 1755. We know that Joseph Higgs was the miller in the 1830s (18). Lord Wrottesley had the present substantial brick mill building erected in 1854 to serve the needs of the village, the district and his estates. Early tenants were James Whitmore and Alfred Jones, but it is the name of Summerton that is synonymous with Trysull Mill. They had been millers since the 1500s. My good friend Harry Brown has been kind enough to supply much of the following information; his mother, Florrie, was one of the children of Alfred and Frances Summerton, who dominated the life and activity at Trysull Mill in the first half of the twentieth century (19).

The mill comprised of far more than the corn and flour mill. Behind it was a large pond, fed by the leat,

Fig. 34   Trysull Mill and yard, 1920s

so that a good head of water could be kept. An adjustable sluice supplied a 12-foot diameter breastshot wheel, which drove the axles and pulleys required to turn the threshing machines, hoist the sacks of grain to the milling floor and work the three pairs of millstones. Between Seisdon and Trysull the river valley has less of a gradient than formerly, so a breastshot wheel (one that is rotated by the falling water striking buckets/paddles at – or just above –

halfway up the wheel's edge) was used. This made the best of the 'fall' available, whilst also using the force of the moving water. This was much more efficient than an undershot wheel. The mill's finished product was either cattle feed or flour. Mr Beards, who worked on Manor Farm, Lower Penn, in the war years, regularly took the horse and cart, laden with oats to be ground into cattle feed at the mill (20).

Across Church Lane was the bakery, which supplied the district with crusty bread, whilst the blacksmith's shop was adjacent to the bridge. Lord Wrottesley had fallen into the Smestow in 1848, horse and all, as there was no parapet to the seven-arch bridge. It was replaced with the present structure in 1852 (21). The site also contained stables and tackle sheds, whilst osier beds completed the rural scene.

In October 1929, the outlying and southerly portions of the Wrottesley estates, some 1500 acres and a quarter of the whole, were offered for sale at the Victoria Hotel in Wolverhampton (22). Alfred had died in July of that year, but Frances Maria, the sitting tenant, bought the mill complex. She continued the trade of threshing and milling corn and baking bread. By this time she was using lorries and vans to transport the goods. Farmers would also bring their own corn to be threshed. Electricity replaced water power about 1940. One wonders if, had the mill pond and fleams had been kept, whether we would by now have installed turbines to produce electricity for the village. By the early 1950s, though, corn milling and flour production had ceased.

Frances died in 1954. At that time her estate included:

> *'the mill house with half an acre, valued at £3000: 13.5 acres of agricultural land, including the mill pool, osier beds and rough pasture, farm buildings and threshing mill, worth £3600; almost 4 acres of land in Trysull (£225); 30.5 acres of agricultural land at Seisdon (£1800); and properties at Bradmore (£1675), at Swan Bank (£150), together with a builder's yard valued at £250'* (23).

Her estate was shared equally by two of her sons, Leonard Gordon and Arnold, who gave the cricket pitch to the village. In 1956 Arnold bought out his brother's share of the Mill House, whilst the Mill and the surrounding 13 acres were sold to Messrs LH and D Lowe for £3250. In 1957 Leonard bought out his brother's share in the osier beds for £164. Connie their sister went to join Arnold in the Mill House. Her Madeira cake and strawberry jam were family favourites and Trysull specialities. Many older residents still remember Connie as their kindly Sunday School teacher.

During the seventies and eighties further sales were made. The blacksmith's shop was sold for £1951, whilst in May 1978 Connie and Arnold, already elderly, left the Mill house. It was sold for £30,750 to the Lowes, who further developed the sandpits at this time (24).

In the early eighties the Lowes put the mill up for sale. It was purchased by Mr and Mrs Tomlinson, who tastefully restored and converted it into a home, with kitchen and living quarters on the first floor and bedrooms on the second and third. The ground floor was kept for the mill machinery and for storage (25). The bake house and stables were separately sold and converted into homes.

When the wind is in the west and there is a rush of water and urgency in the air, spare a thought for Alfred and Frances Summerton, one-time millers at this principal mill of the Smestow Valley. Their job done, they lie at rest in Trysull churchyard.

(1) *Memories of Penn and District. Angus Dunphy. 1988. P79-83; Out And about in Penn. Angus Dunphy. 1990. P79-80.*

(2) *Seisdon Rural District Official Guide. 1973. P25.*

(3) *Various Trysull and Seisdon Parish Magazines.*

(4) *The Past in the Pipeline- Archaeology of the Esso Midline. The Trust for Wessex Archaeology and   Esso.1968.*

(5) *See sketch by David Leverton.*

(6) *SHC Vol IV (i). 1883. P52.*

(7) *Trysull and Seisdon Parish Magazine, March 2000. Parish Mills. Neil E Dean. P9-10*

(8) *Whites Staffordshire History, Gazetteer and Directory. 1851. P209.*

(9) *VCH Vol 20. P187*

(10) *VCH Vol 20. P185.*

(11) *The Pleistocene geology of the area north and west of Wolverhampton. AV Morton. 1973. Philosophical Transactions of the Royal Society of London Vol 265 No 868. P255.*

(12) *A Short Guide to Trysull Village. 1993. ALU Unwin.*

   Mr Unwin has also produced "A Walk about Seisdon".

(13) *Angus Dunphy's Penn. Dulston press. 1987. P124.*

(14) *Domesday Book -Staffordshire. Phillimore.1976. P250a.*

(15) *VCH Vol 20 P192.*

(16) *SHC Vol 12 part 1. 1891. P150-1*

(17) *SHC Vol 17. 1890. P17-18.*

(18) *White's Staffordshire History, Gazetteer and Directory. 1834. P291.*

(19) *Mr Harry Brown. Lower Penn.*

(20) *Mr P Beards. Pennfields.*

(21) *Penn to Paper. Angus Dunphy. 1996. P97-8.*

(22) *Sale Catalogue of the Southern Portion of the Wrottesley Estate . Lot 16. 1929.*

(23) *ibid 19.*

(24) *ibid 19.*

(25) *Express and Star. Homes Guide. Saturday April 28, 1984.*

Fig. 35

TRYSULL MILL TO HEATH MILL PART 1

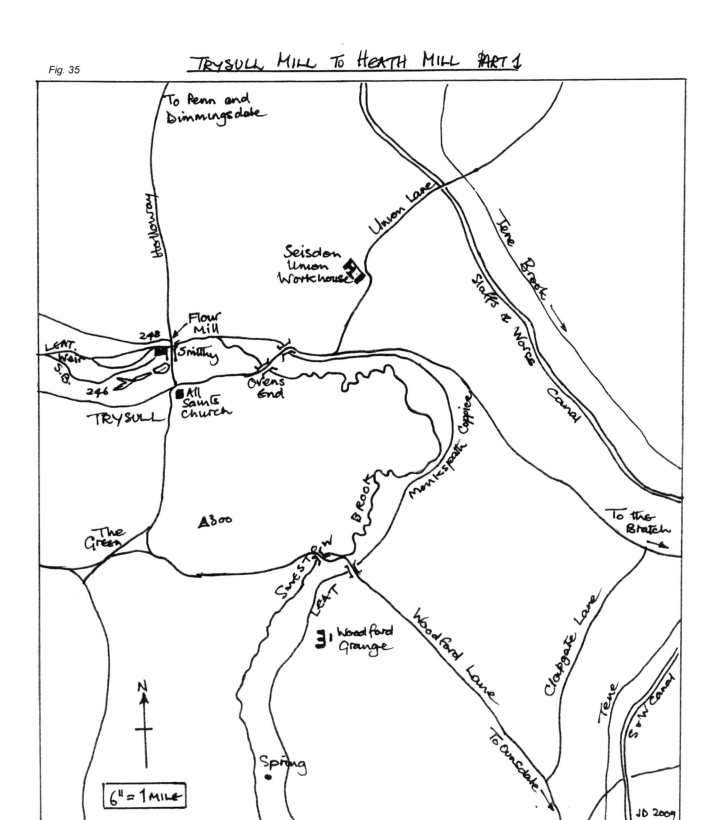

To Penn and Dimmingsdale

Holloway

Union Lane

Tene Brook

Seisdon Union Workhouse

Staffs & Worcs Canal

Flour Mill

248

Smithy

LEAT Weir S.G.

246

Ovens End

All Saints Church

TRYSULL

The Green

A800

Monkspath Coppice

Swestow Brook

LEAT

To the Bratch

Clapgate Lane

Woodford Grange

Woodford Lane

Tene

S & W Canal

N

To Onscote

Spring

6" = 1 MILE

JD 2009

56

Between Seisdon and Trysull the Smestow has followed a more or less straight course and fallen some twenty feet, on its journey to meet the Stour at Prestwood. The depth of the river is fairly even across its bed. On its next journey from Trysull Mill to Smestow Bridge, which carries the B4176, it also falls some twenty feet. However, part of its one and a half mile course is characterised by meander bends. The inside banks are heavily eroded by the force of the deep water, whilst the shallows are found on the outsides of the bends, where sand, silt and rounded pebble stones are deposited.

The Smestow flows underneath Trysull Holloway, the three-span cast iron road bridge dating from 1852. Today's bridge carries notice of the Motor Car Act of 1903, which informs the traveller that it cannot carry an axle weight greater than four tons. The notice concludes, 'by order of Staffordshire County Council, Walter H Cheadle, Surveyor'. The river flows in an easterly direction and the fleam left the main channel on its long journey to the pool at Heath Mill, Wombourne.

Fig. 36   Trysull–Ebstree Rd bridge, and attached notice (inset)

At Ovens End the Wombourne road crosses the Smestow on a bridge of 1805. It was built at the time of Dr Henry Jesson, churchwarden, Overseer of the Poor and resident of Trysull Manor House. It was here that a tragedy occurred in 1883. At the inquest held by the coroner, Mr WH Phillips of Penn, it was reported that William Humphreyson, aged fifty, a labourer, had been

Fig. 37   Ovens End bridge

found drowned. From the evidence available it transpired that Humphreyson had been drinking at The Bell on Wednesday evening the 14th March. He left the hostelry at about 10.00pm the worse for wear, and began his walk home to Ounsdale. Finger marks in the river bank showed that he had been unable to scramble out. The jury declared a verdict of accidental drowning, but drew the parish surveyor's attention to the dangerous state of the bridge sides, adjacent to the spot where William met his death (1).

The fleam passes underneath the Wombourne Road at the sharp bend before Union Lane is reached. High up on the river terrace are the remains of the workhouse, that most hated of Victorian institutions. It was built as a result of the Poor Law Amendment Act of 1834, which required parishes to group together in setting up a Board of Guardians, with the task of making workhouse life more unpleasant than the poverty outside. There were rules concerning diet, the separation of the sexes, building design, and expectation of work to be done. Seisdon's Union of parishes, together with Rudge, built the structure up high on the river terrace, where its visibility was a warning to all in the district that life outside was infinitely better for both the poor and the rates. It was opened in 1860. With the start of Old Age Pensions for those over 70 in 1908, living conditions for the aged poor improved. By 1921 the number of inmates had been reduced to 75. Despite the workhouse's closure in 1936, its subsequent use as an egg-packing station and the demolition of the main buildings in 1965, the eeriness of the Union remains *(2)*. Folklore tells of a phantom rider, who gallops across the countryside destroying fences and gates and leaving a trail of destruction. No-one ever sees him, but some claim he was one of the last inmates, others that he is responsible for the blue lights supposedly seen in the workhouse windows. A few hold the view that he was getting his own back on the Board of Guardians, some of whom were farmers. There are those, however, who know the true story of this 1950s vandalism… On a lighter note, local farmers complained that they could not keep a decent set of clothes on their respectable scarecrows, as they stood in the path of the tramps who made their way to the workhouse for a night's lodging!

Beyond the workhouse on the way to Orton hamlet is Awbridge, with its humpbacked canal bridge, the copings of which are supported on nine brick-built pillars. This is the prettiest bridge on the Staffordshire and Worcestershire Canal. On the far side is Lower Penn's Tene Brook which fed Heath Mill pool. The quiet traveller can watch the kingfisher at work between bridge, lock and brook.

The Smestow and its fleam turn south and enter the delightfully wooded water meadows known as Monkspath Coppice. It is not named after the inmates of Woodford Grange, a house originally owned by the Cluniac Priory of Dudley (1161), itself a cell of Wenlock. Woodford was a farm above the fording place on the Smestow. Its workers are unlikely to have been monks, but they would have attended the parish church on Sundays. A direct footpath still links the Grange to All Saints, but this does not go through Monkspath Coppice. Tony Unwin, the Seisdon and Trysull historian, has suggested the name's likely derivation: he reminds us that there was a Tudor family in the parish called Mempas and surmises that Mempas's Copy became Mumpasses Coppy and with further changes became today's attractive name *(3)*.

Whilst the Trysull-Wombourne Road heads for the Bratch, Woodford Lane cuts across the brook and the now dried-up fleam. To the north of the bridge the river has meandered across the meadows. In Tudor times yeomen were encouraged to grow hemp, a plant growing up to five feet in height. There is evidence that it was grown in Trysull *(4)*. One wonders if the stems were laid in these pools to rot or 'ret', or whether the stretch between Trysull and Seisdon was preferred? After retting, the exposed fibres were scraped and combed. Once dried the fibres were twisted into a thick thread before being woven into a coarse cloth.

Woodford was an extra parochial unit of about 200 acres which after the dissolution of the monasteries was eventually acquired by the Lee family. Mary Lee married Sir Walter Wrottesley in 1568 and the property remained with this family until the sale of their southern estates in 1929. The fleam crossed one of Woodford's drives, as does the footpath to Poolhouse. South of Woodford the ground has been extensively quarried for glacial sands and gravels and the land surface considerably reduced. This is also true of the valley itself, for at Smestow Bridge were large sand quarries and a concrete pipe works *(5)*. An industrial estate now occupies the site.

The fleam crossed underneath Poolhouse Road and fed the extensive Heath Mill pool. The 1808 enclosure award map shows not one but two pools – the 'New Pool' (which is the pond shown on the adjacent sketch map), and an equally large 'Old Pool' lying immediately to the south. It is likely therefore that the fleam from the Smestow and the New Pool date from the later years of the eighteenth century. Doubtless its construction heralded a time of increasing demand at the forge, when a greater supply and increased fall of water would have assisted production. The Georgian-era Heath House would have been the residence of the forgemasters. The now demolished Pool House Cottage was probably built to house a labourer, whose job it would have been to keep the fleam free and flowing.

Fig. 38

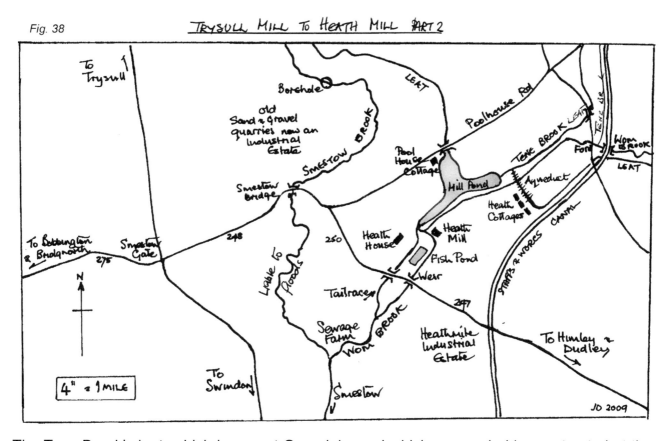

The Tene Brook's leat, which began at Ounsdale, and which was probably constructed at the same time as the Smestow fleam, was a second source of water for the mill pond. A third source came from the Wom Brook. A leat left the main channel east of the canal, passed underneath it and ran through the meadow, before turning northwards on an iron aqueduct (known to generations of Wombourne children as the 'truffin', as they balanced their way across it) *(6)*. The water then joined the Tene's leat just short of the mill pond. So Heath Mill had three sources of water supply – the Smestow, Tene and Wom Brooks. The construction works of pool and fleams was considerable, and it is to the credit of the eighteenth-century engineers that they graded the channel and flows correctly.

At the western end of the millponds lay Heath Mill. Quite when it started is open to debate. We know that William Wollaston purchased a mill from John Grey, Lord of the Manor of Orton, in the twenty-sixth year of Elizabeth I's reign (1584). This mill was probably the one sold to Sir Hugh Wrottesley in 1601. He converted it to a hammer mill. This may well be Heath Forge *(7)*. The date fits approximately with the development of Grange Furnace in Lower Penn, which was owned by the Wollastons and which subsequently sent much pig iron to Heath Forge, so it is probable that the two plants were set up to complement each other.

Heath Forge developed and used the waters from the Y-shaped pool. Iron forges needed a large supply of water, as they took pig iron from the furnace and changed it into bar iron through many processes, each of which required waterpower to drive the bellows or to power the hammers. Plot, writing in 1686, gives us a picture of the processes that were undertaken at the forge:

> *'From the furnaces they bring sows and pigs of iron to the forges, which are of two sorts, but commonly standing together under the same roof - the finery and the chafery. Both are open hearths upon which they place great heaps of coal, which are blown by bellows. In the finery the pigs and sows are melted down as thin as lead, when the metal in an hour thickens by degrees into a lump, which they call a loop. It is taken to the hammer, raised by the motion of a water wheel, it is beaten into a thick square which is called a half bloom. It is reheated and beaten and worked into a bloom - a square with knobs on both ends, the larger knob being called a mocket head and the smaller one an ancony end. The ancony end of the bloom is then heated for a quarter of an hour in the chafery forge, before being brought to the hammer and there beaten into a bar. The larger end is reheated twice before it can be wrought under the hammer into bars.' (8)*

The bars were then sold and carried to the slitting mill, in Heath Forge's case usually to the Hyde at Kinver.

Dud Dudley, an illegitimate son of Lord Dudley and Elizabeth Tomlinson, a collier's daughter, is popularly accepted as the inventor of smelting iron using coal instead of charcoal. Modern research suggests that his claims of success were ill-founded *(9)*. What is certain is that he can be credited with keeping alive the quest of finding a solution to the dependence of the iron industry on dwindling supplies of charcoal and that commodity's dependence on woodland stocks. His book *Metallum Martis (10)*, published in 1665, looks back over the previous 47 years. He tells of his first success at smelting iron using coke and his subsequent patent. He mentions the four forges of Cradley, Swin, Heath and Greenes and tells us what Plot was later to write down, that 'they barred [made into bars] all or most of their iron with pit cole'.

The seventeenth-century story of Heath Forge is closely connected with the Foley family: Richard, his third son Thomas, and his third son Philip. Thomas took over the Foley iron interests in the 1650s and created an integrated system of iron production for furnace, forge and slitting mill in the Smestow and Stour valleys, which largely guaranteed that supplies for each process were available. Philip took over a considerable number of furnaces, forges and slitting mills from his father in 1669. He kept detailed accounts books, and from these he was able to monitor the value and profitability of individual plants. We know that he paid Sir Walter Wrottesley £42 rent for the Heath site up to the year ending Michaelmas 1669. Richard Grey (Gray) ran the Heath, Swin and Greenes Forges for Philip. The inter-relationship between the industrial sites is clearly shown. 60 tons 4 cwt 2 qt 20lbs of pig iron were supplied to the Heath in that year from Coven and Wombridge (Telford) furnaces, whilst Richard Grey's account was credited with £40-15s-10½p for carrying pigs to Heath Mill. Likewise his account was paid a sum of £28-0-3, for carrying Heath's bar iron to the Hyde. The tonnage sent was 71. The Heath did send, on occasion, some of its bar to other slitting mills such as Bustleholme *(11)*.

The annual output of Heath Forge in the 1670s was around one hundred tons of bar iron. To produce this it required around two hundred tons of coal and one hundred and sixty tons of pig. The output, transported to the slitting mills lower down the valley, would be turned into rods for onward transmission to the cottage-based nail industry.

By 1674 Philip Foley had enough evidence to assess the profitability of each plant. He described, in glowing terms, the forges of Heath, Swin and Greenes as:

'very beneficial works being well watered and soe convenient to Grange for pig, and ye market for sale, and ye wayes good which save an abundance in carriage. They are also in very good repayre and have little or no watercourse rents to charge or incumber the owner. They lie near to pit coal for drawing out iron and workmens fires as any workes can... And here are woods to supply these works with charcoles.' (12)

But were they that profitable? In the years between 1650 and 1673 Heath Forge's annual profit varied from between £105 to £354. The annual profit in the period 1669-1673 ranged from £235 to £154. He leased the three forges, together with Grange Furnace, to Sir Clement Clerke and Alderman John Foorth. They ran into financial difficulties and the business was re-leased. Whether he did this to increase his return, or to free up capital to repay his father, or to cover the high cost of importing high quality pigs from his brother Paul's furnaces in the Forest of Dean is open to debate *(13)*. In the 1690s the Powells operated the forge.

During this period Wombourne Heath lay on the direct route from London to Anglesey and Ireland. Ogilby's maps of 1675 show the route from London to Birmingham, and then via Dudley, Gornalwood and Himley to Wombourne Common. The Heath was on the London Road. There was then no bridge at Smestow Bridge, merely a ford, which must have made life difficult in times of Smestow flood. Beyond the tollgate at

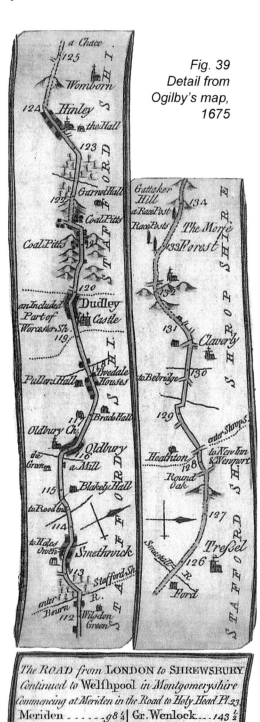

Fig. 39
Detail from Ogilby's map, 1675

61

Smestow Gate the mail coach reached Heathton, cut through Morfe Forest, and travelled on to Bridgnorth, Great Wenlock, Shrewsbury and Welshpool.

There is one further reference to Heath Forge during this period. In 1678 James Illingworth published an account of the man whose hands and legs rotted off *(14)*. The account tells us that John Downing lived near Heath Forge.

For many years in the eighteenth century up until the 1780s, Richard Jordan of the Grange Furnace family operated Heath Forge. The Staffordshire and Worcestershire Canal served the forge from the 1770s. Barges docked at Heath Wharf (Crane Cottages), which was situated between Giggetty Bridge and Brickbridge (Wombourne Bridge). A number of cottages were built on the wharf. Three more down the track on the way to the forge went by the delightful name of 'Tea Kettle Row' *(15)*. They were probably not very delightful to live in. The forge was in operation until at least 1814. By 1825 it was producing iron rods. Richard Southall and John Hart of the Heath Forge Company regularly requested Messrs Elwell & Co., nailmasters with warehouses in Sedgley and Wombourne, to take their wares and pay their bills *(16)*. Both concerns seemed to be suffering from a downturn in trade and cashflow problems. It is therefore no surprise to learn that the date stone of 1827, on the new mill, showed the site had reverted to corn milling. The initials 'Sr J W' witnessed it had been built for Sir John Wrottesley (who was ninth baronet, first baron, succeeded 1792, died 1841).

The mill, of four storeys, was driven by a large overshot wheel, which was contained in a lean-to on the northwest wall. The eighteenth-century 'New Pool', which was constructed on higher

Fig. 40   Heath Mill, 1827

ground than the lower pool, allowed this more efficient wheel type to be used. The mill's gearing system drove three pairs of grindstones, with a set in reserve in case of breakdown. For much of the century the Jones family were millers here; Eli in 1834, Whitmore by 1851 and John and Alfred by 1872. When the mill was put up for sale in 1929 it was offered together with Heath House, Heath Mill Farm and Heath Cottages. The parcel of land was about 70 acres. Mr A Nock was the tenant of the mill. The mill house had dining and breakfast rooms, kitchen, back kitchen, pantry and cellars, together with six bedrooms, box room and bathroom *(17)*. The mill, a principal mill of the Smestow valley, and one of three offered for sale by the Wrottesley Estate, continued in operation until just before the Second World War. Mr Nock remained as tenant until the new owner decided to sell in 1936. In actual fact he was there until his tenancy ran out on one of the farming quarter days – Lady Day 1937 *(18)*. This is probably the date by which milling had ceased.

The New Pool, which was quite shallow, was a favourite winter venue for skating before the Second World War *(19)*. Generations of Wombourne folk looked forward to the millpond freezing over. Skates were re-sharpened and much village fun was had; ice hockey teams were very much in evidence. In the summers Mr Nock's children and probably others swam in the pool. But war brought dire shortages of food and so it had to be drained and sown with potatoes. The Old Pool had ceased to exist long before this and had been turned into meadow land, and that too was put to good use for grazing. After the war the area we know as Poolhouse was quarried for sand, before the house builders arrived in the 1970s. The mill fell victim to the developers; it and both pools now lie under the Poolhouse Estate. Only the road names on the estate (Millfields, Millers Way and Forge Way) now remind us of this area's former role.

Fig. 41   Millpool, Heath Mill

The soils of Poolhouse and the adjacent areas of the Wom and Smestow Brooks supported a wonderful array of wildflowers, some of which have made it into the estate's road names – The Celandines, Rosebay Grove and Campion Close. May Griffiths reminds us that little purple orchids grew on what is now Marlburn Way and that lady's smock and marsh marigolds grew in the meadow that had been the Old Pool *(20)*.

Below the mill the waters fed the fishpond of the Georgian Heath House, which was fortunately kept by the developers. The stream then fell over a weir/waterfall to the Bridgnorth Road. The planners did not keep this attractive feature, straightening out the brook across the site. Beyond the B4176 the Wom Brook passes through the sewage farm site.

Returning to the Smestow's journey below Woodford Lane there is only one point of interest. This is the 2842-feet borehole, the deepest water well in Britain (21). German workers sank it in 1912. They were probably in the employ of the Earl of Dudley. The group lodged with cottagers in Smestow, Trysull and Wombourne, their presence arousing much suspicion locally. Some say their borehole was an attempt to lower the water table in Baggeridge Colliery, some two miles away. This is unlikely. The Black Country coalfield was largely worked out and Baggeridge was a new venture, on the concealed coalfield, which was then just coming into full production. The borehole sinking was an attempt to find coal west of the Stapenhill and Lloyd House faults and prove that workable coal lay beneath the Triassic sandstones. Seven feet of coal was found at a depth of 2725 feet; the small thickness of coal suggesting that the bore could have passed through a fault. It was thought the seam equated to the 22-feet thick coal seam at Baggeridge (22). The bore lies within the industrial estate and is currently not used, although licensed for the extraction of 13 million gallons annually.

During the Second World War, a rotary quern-stone was dug up by the driver of a steam shovel, to the west of the Smestow Brook between Smestow Bridge and the turnoff for Trysull. This was in the then Messrs. J Cross & Sons sand and gravel quarry. The quern lay in a bed of gravel and was seven to eight feet below the surface of the ground. Experts dated it to between the first century B.C. and the second century A.D., reminding us that the area was peopled and that grain was being grown here for making flour (23).

The confluence of the Smestow and Wom Brooks lies beneath Smestow Bridge. A thirteenth-century deed in the Wodehouse Collection gives an apt description as it describes a grant of land – 'a meadow beginning at a place where the water of Wombourne falls into the water of Tresel' (24). Water voles and otters have now returned to these waters.

(1) Penn to Paper. Angus Dunphy. 1996. P97.

(2) Victoria County History Vol XX. P193.

(3) Trysull and Seisdon Parish Magazine Sept 2001. Tony Unwin. P6-7.

(4) Trysull and Seisdon Parish Magazine Feb 2001. Neil E Dean. P9-10.

(5) A Geography of Lower Penn and Wombourne. Angus Dunphy. 1972. Dudley Teachers' Centre Item 2196. P18.

(6) I am grateful to May Griffiths, Wombourne's Historian, for this information and as always for discussion over all things to do with the parish.

(7) VCH Vol XX. P212.

(8) The Natural History of Staffordshire. Robert Plot. 1686. Chapter 4 v24.

(9) Transactions of the Newcomen Society 1934. RA Mott "Dud Dudley and the Early Coal Industry". P17-37.

(10) Metallum Martis. Dud Dudley. 1665. Bagnall Edition 1854. P35.

(11) Worcestershire Historical Society New series Vol 13. A selection from the records of Philip Foley's Stour Valley Ironworks 1668-74. Editor RG Shafer.

(12) Hereford Record Office. Foley Papers.

(13) Business History Vol 13(1) 1971, P19-38. Genesis and Structure of the Foley Ironworks in Partnership of 1692. RG Shafer.

(14) A Just or Narrative Account of the Man whose Hands and Legs rotted off in

the parish of Kingswinford. Carefully Collected by James Illingworth B.D. 1678.

(15) The Wom Brook Tale. May Griffiths. Extensive document to be placed in Wombourne History Room.

(16) 1825 Letters from the Heath Forge Company to Messrs. Elwell & Co.

(17) Sale particulars of the outlying and southern parts of the Wrottesley Estate. October 23rd, 1929.

(18) Letters to the Black Country Bugle. Mrs Bennett, daughter of Mr Nock.

(19) Information from May Griffiths, Wombourne.

(20) ibid 16.

(21) Penn in Print. Angus Dunphy. 2000. P142-3.

(22) Geology of the country between Dudley and Bridgnorth. HMSO.

(23) Transactions of Shropshire Archaeological Society Vol 52. P117-121.

(24) Historical Collections Staffordshire Vol for 1928. P16 section 10.

Fig. 42

THE TENE BROOK c.1913

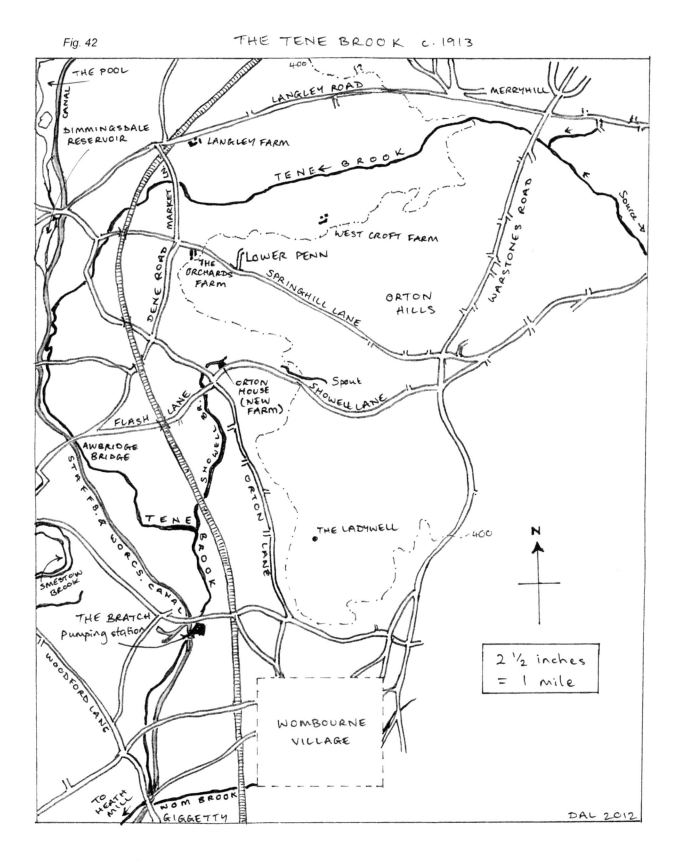

Chapter 10
The Tene Brook

Few in the district know the name of this brook, yet most will know of its existence. Its name means a gathering ground of waters, which is very apt for its drainage basin covers the area to the west of the Colton Hills and Goldthorn Hill. It begins life in many places along the ridge, although its headwaters are not obvious these days as they have vanished into the storm-water sewers. Stand on Goldthorn Hill or in Mount Road in a heavy shower and you can't fail to realise the considerable run-off down towards the Penn Road and beyond. In fact, some of us remember the fun of riding a trolley bus through the swollen storm waters at the junction with Manor Road, in the days when the Penn Road was still single-carriageway

The watercourse first really appears along Woodlands Walk. Another branch is culverted under the A449, before flowing through the allotments between Woodfield Avenue and Wynn Road. This rivulet then crosses Wynn Road and Windsor Avenue, before reaching the playing fields, where it joins the trickle from Woodlands Walk. The brook's volume is swelled from a stream from Pinfold Lane, before a further trickle reaches it from Coalway Road and Pennfields. St Philip's Church, built in 1859, was erected in a field called 'Cloddy Mere', whose waters drained away into this trickle, which reaches the Tene to the south of Warstones School.

Between 1988 and 1991 a modern twin foul- and storm-water sewer of just over a mile in length was constructed along Coalway Road, from the junctions with Woodfield Avenue and New Street. Its purpose was to relieve flooding at times of heavy rains. Additional sections linked Wynn, Leighton and Church Roads and Leasowes Drive to the main line. The seven-foot diameter sewer lies at a depth of 30 feet and has the capacity to shift 15,000 gallons of effluent a minute. About 1000 feet of the tunnel's length was bored by using Channel Tunnel-type excavating machines (1).

Water from the Springhill/Hollybush Lane area of Warstones Road disappears into the storm-water sewer system. Up until the 1990s heavy storms often caused flooding in Warstones Crescent. This has been averted with considerable and ingenious drainage works. A series of tanks and weirs, constructed underground, pond back excess storm water and let it out when the flow is less fierce (2).

The area between Warstones Road and the Library was probably once a medieval homestead moat, which gave the household of a locally important Pennite status and protection. The Tene continues its journey underground through the Warstones Estate, emerging by the side of Highfields School and flowing past Hillcroft Farm. The waters which have been collected from the north bank of the Orton Hills seep into Spring Pool, which itself feeds the Tene. The fields hereabout are called 'Cranmoor', the moor of the cranes. Once this was marsh and it supported the most popular of medieval wildfowl, the heron. In Edward I's day the price of a heron was sixteen pence, a higher sum than that paid for any other wildfowl. Whilst the crane did breed in Britain until the sixteenth century (3), its cousin the heron was often called by the same name. The careful observer can still see herons on Cranmoor.

They stand motionless in the brook until suddenly a sharp downwards jab of the beak announces the bird has caught its dinner. Herons can also be seen braving the winter cold with hunched backs, on one of their traditional 'standing' grounds.

In 1905 Seisdon Rural District Council laid out the Merry Hill sewage works site on land adjacent to the brook and Langley Road. Built to serve the growing population of Bradmore and Merry Hill, it was of no use to Lower Penn as the village lay downstream of the works. After 1932 the plant was extended to meet the fast-growing district of Upper Penn, where 400 houses a year were being built. The storm tanks were unable to cope with the flows in periods of severe flooding and much raw sewage was returned to the watercourse. However, in dry periods as much as 80% of the stream's flow came from the clear treated water returned to the brook by the works *(4)*.

It was left to the Severn Trent Water Authority to solve the capacity issues, when they took over management of the works in 1974. Their solution was to close the sewage farm and pump the effluent to their major works at Barnhurst. Land was therefore released for housing, which we know today as that around Hamble Road/Fareham Crescent.

Between Merry Hill and Ebstree the Tene flows through a broad valley, which it could never have carved. The culprit was glacial meltwater at the end of the last ice age. This generation of Lower Penn residents know the brook as the 'Muddy River', as it traditionally has flooded at Market Lane and again at Penn Halt/Greyhound Lane, as well as at Penstones. Since the 1990s this has largely been averted by the building of a flood meadow dam near to the footpath which joins Dirty Foot Lane with the Warstones Estate. Floodwater is ponded back, to be slowly released through a throttle pipe in the dam's earth wall. At other times cattle can graze the meadow.

In Greyhound Lane is Severn-Trent's Dimmingsdale Waterworks. The sandstones of the Trias extend to a considerable depth and overlie the coal measures which have been downthrown near Baggeridge and which re-appear in the Shropshire Coalfield. The sandstones are pervious and absorb much of the rain that falls. In 1896 the then Wolverhampton Corporation Water Undertaking obtained an order to tap Dimmingsdale's underground water, but it was not proceeded with. However, the opportunity to purchase 16 acres of land for the Dimmingsdale site was taken at the time of the sale of the Duke of Sutherland's Penn Estate in 1917. After the First World War Wolverhampton Corporation's water needs had increased and work started at Dimmingsdale in 1923. The first borehole was sunk to a depth of 1025 feet and completed by 1925. The second borehole, of a similar depth, was completed by 1927, but under test the contractor lost part of his pumping equipment at a depth of 256 feet. It took two years to retrieve. The station buildings (now much reduced) and the employee's houses were then built. The station opened on 28th May 1932 and yielded 3 million gallons of water daily *(5)*.

The Tene cuts underneath Penstone Lane and flows near to Lower Penn's important electricity grid station. At this point it takes the excess canal water from the Dimmingsdale pound. The brook keeps company with the Staffordshire & Worcestershire Canal for the rest of its short journey. At Awbridge, my favourite lock, the babbling brook is seen from the road as it makes for the Bratch.

Between the two locks the Tene attracts a small tributary. This has started life at the spout high up on Showell Bank, flowing down the steep scarp face and through the garden of Rose Cottage, before vanishing underneath the meadows of the Showell Valley. The Showell Brook re-emerged to feed the fish ponds that once existed at New Farm (Orton House). At the Showell/Orton Lanes' crossroads the roadway to Trysull is named Flash Lane. This term refers to the type of flooding which occurs at this spot after heavy thunderstorms, the considerable run-off carrying down the bank much sand/silt and rounded pebble.

The origin of the name Showell comes from Anglo-Saxon and may mean 'Seven Wells', a reference to the water-bearing properties of the sandstones and the numerous springs which occur hereabouts. Some say it means show well. However Duignan prefers the explanation of an ancient enclosure in the forest, where 'shows' or scarecrows on the fences kept the deer out (6). Other Showells and Seven Wells occur in Wolverhampton, near Spring Hill in the Cotswolds and near Cheltenham.

Whilst the next valley at Orton is called 'Hope', which means dry valley, there are numerous springs in the district, including the Ladywell situated high up in the woods. The waters seep towards the Showell Brook, on its journey to join the Tene.

In medieval, Tudor and Stuart times there were mills at Orton. One was probably the forerunner of Heath Mill, which lay in the extensive Orton Liberty. However, the Caldewall or Caldewell (the cold well) Mill and Trigg Mill (7) are also mentioned; they may have been sited in Orton hamlet itself, or more probably at the junction of the Showell Brook with the Tene, where the very modest water supply was greater. The Tene Valley at Awbridge is deep enough to have accommodated a mill pool, but there is no evidence of this.

The Bratch is famous for its three locks and for the 1895 red-brick fairytale castle/waterworks. Here the Tene passes underneath the canal to the western side. The waterworks was built by the Urban District of Bilston. An industrial township, it had relied for its supply firstly on water from local mines, which proved to be an unsuitable source, and then on the Wolverhampton and South Staffordshire Companies. Bilston was keen to gain an independent supply and not to have to pay high charges to other bodies. To this end it began its own scheme at the Bratch in 1892. It took five years to complete, but then served not only the township, but Wombourne, Woodford Grange, Trysull, Seisdon, Himley, Swindon and parts of Coseley. Many villagers' wells in Wombourne and Trysull ran dry, and to compensate the parishes were offered substantial reductions for the piped supply.

Two boreholes were sunk in the close-grained Upper Mottled Sandstone of the Bunter series to a depth of 147 and 141 feet respectively and two 400-ton vertical triple expansion steam engines were installed. Coal was brought in by barge to the wharf. Water was pumped through a pipeline from the Bratch to the high point of Goldthorn Hill, from whence there is a gravity feed to Bilston. The pumping engines have somehow survived and today are known as 'Victoria' and 'Alexandra'. The Bratch is part of Severn-Trent Heritage Estate. In 1990 they approached Mr Len Crane, who with a group of volunteers restored 'Victoria' to working order. This took five years. The engine has been steamed most years since (8).

Demand for water was increasing and Bilston needed to increase its supply and pumping capacity. Well number 2 was deepened to over 640 feet to tap the Bunter Pebble Beds. New pumping equipment, namely two sets of 'Rushton' vertical oil engines of 300bhp – direct-coupled through bevel gearing to two 'Sulzer' vertical turbine pumps, capable of raising 70,000 gallons per hour at 494 feet, including frictional resistances – were installed in 1927. The new pumping house and engines, new 16-inch pipeline to Goldthorn Hill and the reservoir cost £74,000 (9). 'Victoria' and 'Alexandra' were kept as back-up. Whilst The Bratch's smokestack was felled, the castellated building housing the steam engines has survived and is now a grade 2* listed building. The Bratch yields 2 million gallons of water a day.

Flowing south from the Bratch the Tene passes through the Bumblehole, Ounsdale and on to Giggetty, all once famous for their sand beds and their trade with Black Country foundries. After Ounsdale a leat left the brook and flowed in parallel down to Giggetty Bridge. The leat entered one of the arms of Heath Mill's New Pool, as discussed in the previous chapter.

The Tene, after running under Giggetty Lane, joins the Wom, which has flowed across the Longford (Dickies Ford) and entered the water meadows. This area is still liable to flooding. Indeed, May Griffiths, the Wombourne historian, reminds us that the area may have got its name from the gig pits or pools, where the inner stalk of the flax plant was retted (rotted) away, leaving the outer fibres intact for twine or linen manufacture to take place. An alternative, rather darker derivation is 'the area of the gibbet tree'.

For some this last stretch of the Tene is called the Penn Brook, but this is incorrect and misleading. The actual Penn Brook began life on the eastern side of the Colton Hills and became the Wom when it entered the ancient parish of Wombourne at the Wodehouse Mill pool. It is fitting that the Tene, which started life on the western side of the Colton hills, should join forces with the Wom on its last half mile before it tumbles down into the Smestow below Heathmill.

(1) Information from the then Wolverhampton MB Council, Technical Services Department.

(2) ibid 1

(3) Penn in Print, 2000. Angus Dunphy. P67-75.
   The Crane has successfully been re-introduced into Norfolk in small numbers since the 1980s.

(4) ibid 3.

(5) Wolverhampton Corporation Water Undertaking- Souvenir of the Inauguration of the New Dimmingsdale Waterworks- 10th October, 1932 by His worship, The Mayor of Wolverhampton, Alderman Joseph Haddock, JP.

(6) Staffordshire Placenames, 1902, Duignan. P135-6.

(7) VCH. P212.

(8) Smestow Vale Grapevine May and June 2008; May and July 2009.

(9) Water and The Water Engineer March 1928, P101-105; April 1928, P153-8.

Fig. 43

THE PENN BROOK FROM SOURCE

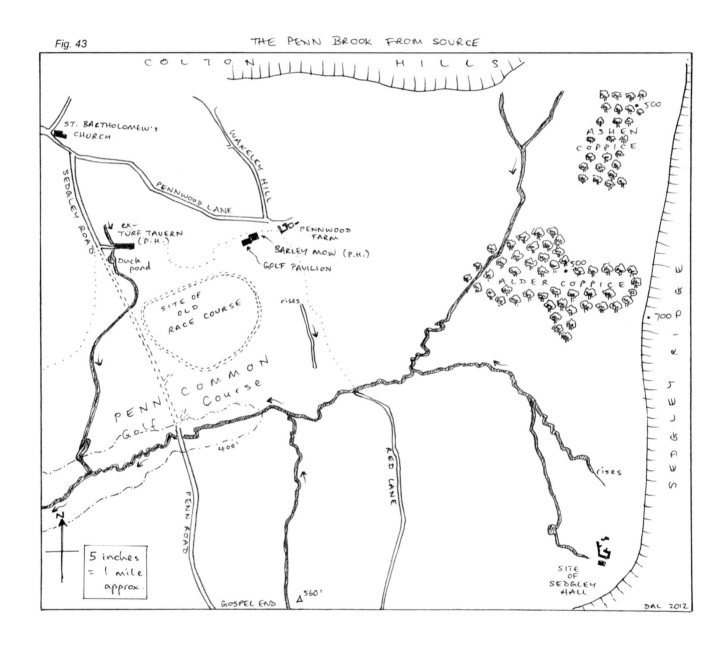

The Penn Brook, one of the main tributaries of the Smestow Brook, rises through a series of springs in farmland beyond Penn Common. It falls some 300 feet in five miles, passing through some pretty countryside and the village of Wombourne, before joining the Smestow beyond Heathmill. Once its waters drove up to half a dozen mills of varying descriptions and at one site produced electricity. Its potential to drive a generator or two today lies untapped.

The Penn Brook rises in the natural amphitheatre created by the heights of the Colton Hills, Goldthorn Park and Sedgley's Northway. The Ramada Park (Hall) hotel overlooks the valley. In the eighteenth century its central building called 'The Lantern' lit the way at dusk for boys returning to their Catholic boarding school, from a day out on the Common. The Trent-Severn watershed passes close by the building; everything beneath it on the southern side flows by way of Penn, Wom, Smestow and Stour to the Severn and the Bristol Channel.

A little distance below today's hotel is Park Coppice and it is here that the infant Penn Brook springs forth. Another rivulet rises a field away and once the two join they flow south. Their waters are swelled by a brook draining the former farmlands of Hickmerelands and Sedgley Hall (housing estates). This joins the Penn Brook shortly before the waters reach Penn Common at the Red Lane end. When the Penn Brook's flow is low, fifty percent of its water comes from the treated water returned to it from the Gospel End sewage works *(1)*. The brook now turns west and enters a deep channel in which it lies for most of its journey across the Common.

A further small stream joins from Gospel End, before the Lloyd Roberts building and Mr Millard's 1860 brewery buildings *(2)* are reached in the dip of Penn Common Road. The road is quite new, being cut in 1870. The brewery never really succeeded as the heavy drays had to be pulled up a steep gradient, whichever way they went. At this time the Common was described as a morass in winter. Penn Golf Club have drained it, but the many springs, now channelled, flow from its slopes and duck pond (below the Turf Cottages) to further swell the brook. The south-west corner is characterised by ravines, which like the bed of the main river saw downcutting at the end of the last ice age. If you pick up pebbles on the Common they are rounded and smooth, showing that once they were carried by glacial meltwater.

The Domesday survey of 1086 *(3)* credits Upper Penn with a mill, valued at two shillings. Quite where the mill was is open to conjecture, but a good bet is on the stretch of the Penn Brook somewhere along the bottom of the Common near to the footbridge. This takes the walker from Gospel End towards Chamberlains Lane. A mill is still shown on a map of 1797, which charts the proposals of John Adams. He was tasked with carrying out a survey on behalf of the Staffordshire and Worcestershire Canal Navigation Company, with the aim of increasing its water supply, and thereby making the operation of the locks more efficient in times of water shortage. His scheme was to dam four ravines at the bottom of the Common and to collect the water, before allowing it to flow via the Penn/Wom Brook to the canal. He planned to buy fifteen acres of the Common at £10 an acre; this cost, together with the dam construction between £46 and £84 per dam, required a total outlay of some £400. Fortunately the canal company did not proceed with the scheme *(4)*.

The history of Penn Common, or Pennwood as it was known to generations of Pennites, began with the villagers using it as manorial waste. By the early nineteenth century it was the venue for Penn Races. Later in the century there were several proposals to build long distance railways across its surface and to mine coal from beneath its turf. In the Second World War it provided the site for a heavy artillery battery and a searchlight crew, whose aim was to bring down enemy bombers. After the 3.7-inch guns left, the Americans came to the camp at the top of the Common, whilst post D-Day Italian prisoners of war were billeted there. From Victorian times until the 1950s Penn Common was one of Wolverhampton's playgrounds. Families looked forward to a day out. Teas were readily available from one of the many cottages or from the Turf tea rooms and the shops on Sedgley Road. There were also several beer houses: The Turf Tavern, the Barley Mow, The Malt Shovel and the Old Stag's Head. Two of these remain as popular watering holes.

Fig. 44   THE PENN BROOK FROM THE COMMON TO THE WODEHOUSE

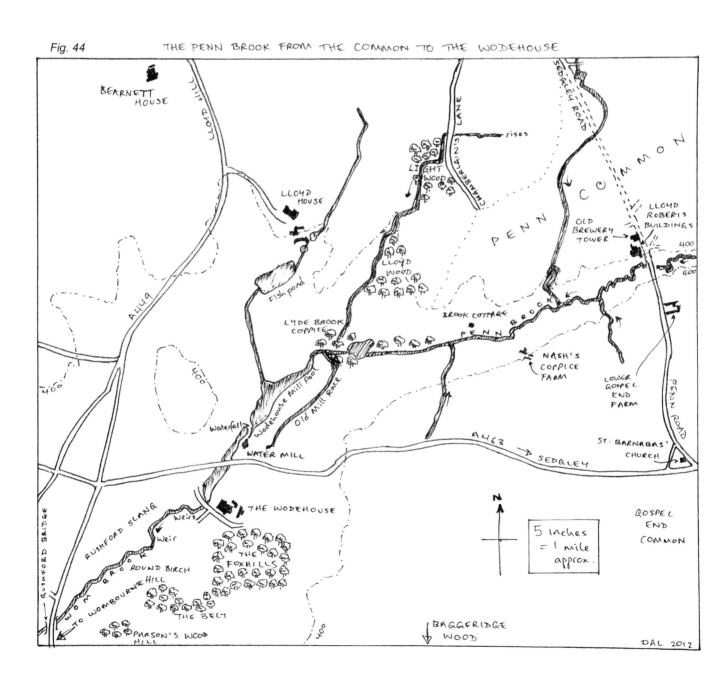

Fig. 45
Penn Common

By the time Brook Cottage is reached the brook has considerable force and it's a foolish man that tries to cross the wooden footbridge in times of severe flood. One of the few remaining arched red-brick bridges over a brook on the Smestow system is to be found at Brook Cottage. It would have carried the cartway running from Chamberlains Lane up to Gospel End, in the days before Penn Common Road was cut. The southern bank was once covered by Nash's Coppice, part of Baggeridge Wood, cleared for the war effort and never replanted. This area was known pre-war as the Little Wood and was much loved for its beauty. The brook continues its journey through pleasant farmland.

Before it reaches the Wodehouse Mill pool the underlying rocks change from the red marls and sandstones of the coal measures to Wombourne's Triassic sandstones. In Lyde Brook Coppice the stream of the same name swells Penn Brook's flow. There was a mill in this area called Ludes Mill in 1458 and it would have been built to take advantage of the waters from both brooks. The Lyde Brook has begun life on the lands known as Penn Moor, which lie adjacent to Vicarage Road and Penn Hall. The use of the name 'moor' is no coincidence, for these lands, like those of the Common and Hickmerelands, have had to be drained with deep ditches. The waters gather and flow via Light Wood, which is a picture at bluebell time, before passing alongside the pheasantry in Lloyd Wood. The Penn Brook enters the once extensive Wodehouse Mill pool, which is suffering from silting and vegetation growth. Pools require cleaning every forty years or so. The last occasion this was done was in 1972 *(5)*.

A second brook rises on Hannoke's Moor. The name in its written form goes back to at least 1300. In 1610 Thomas Burnett sold it to Francis Wodehouse *(6)*. In the mid 1950s, Miss Shaw-Hellier generously gave five and a half acres to the Cheshire Homes Foundation. It is known to many as Ferguson's Common; the name reflects the annual Lady Day tenant of the Lloyd Estate at Lloyd Farm, Neil Ferguson. He farmed these lands from the 1880s until the estate was sold in 1901. The name is not a corruption of 'Macpherson', though George Macpherson, an ironmaster, resided at The Lloyd in the early twentieth century. This brook flows via the Lloyd House fish pond to join the mill pool. The fish pond, which is also suffering from silting, takes the drainage from the A449(T) *(7)*.

Up until 1934 Penn Common lay in Upper Penn parish. Local boundary changes saw Upper Penn vanish into Wolverhampton, with the Common being transferred to Wombourne parish. Up until that date Lower Penn parish stretched down to the mill pool, via a narrow neck of land that we know as Putley or Bearnett. This area, too, went into Wombourne. At the mill pool the brook changes its name from the Penn to the Wom Brook.

The Wodehouse Mill and farm buildings, which form part of the Wodehouse Estate, lie beneath the brick-lined dam. The farmhouse is early eighteenth century, but there has been a mill on this site for many centuries. The Victoria County History points to the fact that the nature of milling changed over time, from fulling (in 1570) to the milling of corn by the 1670s *(8)*. Cooksey and Cooksey also mention a blade mill on this site in the 1690s *(9)*. An important news headline in 1814 was the burning down of the corn mill. It was probably as a result of an arson attack, as a reward was offered for information leading to the conviction of person/s responsible *(10)*.

The re-engineered workings of the present Wodehouse Mill date from 1840, as is noted in the castings. The overshot mill wheel of eight spokes is made from two castings, which made assembly far easier in the confined space available. Bolted together, they still carry the rusting paddles. The diameter of this large mill wheel is 17 feet and the width is 3 feet 5 inches. The wheel came from G and R Turton of Kidderminster and was installed by John Bate, millwright, of Himley (11). The axle connects it to a cast pit wheel, which has 400 'teeth'. To convert the horizontal motion into a vertical plane the cogs of the pit wheel intermesh with the 144 teeth of the wallower, which was also cast in two halves and is secured around the octagonal upright shaft (12). The wallower thereby causes this vertical shaft to rotate. As it has fewer teeth

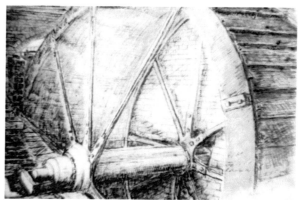

Fig. 46   Wodehouse waterwheel

than the pit wheel the speed of the rotation of the shaft is increased by a ratio of 2.8:1. The shaft runs up through the building and as it revolves, so too does the 120-teeth spur wheel which is attached. This connects with the stone nuts, which drive a pair of Derbyshire burrs. The spur wheel, like the wallower, rotates at about 2.8 times as fast as the speed of the axle, and as it drives the small stone nuts their speed is again greatly increased, making for efficient milling – in some mills the ratios were much higher. There are two pairs of millstones; one of 51 inches diameter, the other of 45 inches. They were supplied by Kay and Hilton of Liverpool (13). Each stone weighs about 30cwts (14). There is also a small crown wheel on the shaft, which drove the machinery for the sack hoists.

Fig. 47   Wodehouse pit wheel

The mill building is of three storeys, but it has four floors! At the base is the ground floor with pit wheel and wallower. Above is the stone floor where the milling took place. Above this is the sack floor, where sacks of corn were stored. In the attic is the service floor. Sacks of grain, attached to a moving chain, were brought up to this level through the trapdoors on each floor. From here the grain was tipped into chutes, which fed the hoppers, which in turn supplied the millstones.

The building was probably extended in 1840, as the joint line down the brickwork shows. The mill wheel is

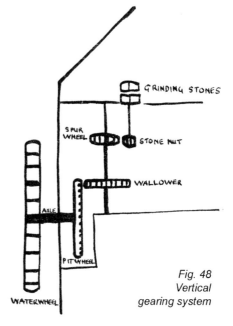

Fig. 48
Vertical
gearing system

sited in this smaller northerly part. The water feed was via a pipe, which filled a header tank up on the sack floor. This gives an indication of the height of the retaining dam wall behind the building. Water was fed onto this pitchback overshot wheel slightly below the crest, causing it to revolve in a reverse direction. On the top service floor there is evidence, in this smaller part of the mill, to suggest there was once a kiln or grain-drying facility.

Before leaving this important mill it should be noted that there is a second, smaller waterwheel, which is situated in a small building behind the mill. The diameter of this overshot wheel is 8 feet and its width 2 feet 8 inches. This drove a chaff cutter and a root pulper in the lower farm buildings. The water feed was via a long mill race, which ran parallel to the mill pond and by a 10-inch pipe. This wheel also drove a pump and generated electricity (15). Water was pumped onto the hill behind the Wodehouse, and then gravity-fed to the estate and to a fountain in the House Pool (16).

The last millers at the Wodehouse were the farm bailiffs, the Elliots. Henry, the father, was the bailiff here in 1924. He took over from William Weaver, who was preceded by Thomas Walters, whilst in 1851 the miller was William Peakman (or Pakeman) (17). The adjacent sketch is of Mr Len Elliot showing a group of Lower Gornal school children around the mill and farm in the 1960s. The almost daily milling of oats and barley for cattle continued until 1976, making the Wodehouse Mill the last one working in our district.

Fig. 49
Mr. Elliot and school visit, Wodehouse Farm

Water from both mill wheels was returned to the main stream via brick-lined tunnels. A spillway from the mill pond goes into a circular brick fish trap, before entering the small pool (again very silted) before the water enters the long slender House Pool stretched from the front of the farmhouse to the Wodehouse. This pool was recently cleared of silt (18).

The origin of the name of Wodehouse is found in its pronunciation – 'Woodhouse'. The house is still surrounded by trees. It is a private house and home and therefore not open to the public. At its core is a medieval timber-framed house dating from about 1350, but its site is at least one hundred years older. The Wodehouse and its grounds have evolved, been altered and added to over the centuries. Whilst there are many interesting features, one thing is special: that the house has apparently never been sold. William the Cook was granted land in Wodehouse Lane in the period 1176-1189 and he added other lands in Wombourne to the family holdings. William Wood, who succeeded to the properties in the 1240s, may have been the first to occupy the site. His son took the name Walter de la Wodehouse and the house took its name from this family. The house passed, by descent, marriage, mortgage and friendship, through the Woodhouses/Wodehouses, Helliers, Shaws, Shaw-Helliers and today is the property of Mr John and Mrs Carolyn Phillips. Through their kindness they have opened their house and grounds regularly over thirty years, to support a range of national and local charities (19). The Wom Brook has been used to enhance the setting of the house and gardens. They are terraced down to the House Pool, whilst the driveway to the house runs across its dam, below which is a small pool.

The brook enters Rushford Slang and flows towards Rushford Bridge, which dates from 1801. It carried the Wolverhampton to Kidderminster turnpike. The present dual carriageway replaced this part of the highway as the through route. However, the name Rushford suggests an early fording place. A document in the Wodehouse collection gives the early spelling of Riseford (20). It is an apt description for the streams which flow off the South Staffordshire plateau, which with heavy rain quickly and substantially increase their rate of flow and depth. Somewhere at Rushford, in the late thirteenth century a fish pond was abandoned, but the reason is not known (21).

Modern day Wombourne is blessed with the Wom Brook Walk, which provides a green transect across the village and which is both a linear park and a wildlife habitat. The walk extends from Rushford Bridge to Pool House. My village of Dinas Powys in the Vale of Glamorgan can look on with envy, for it too has a pleasant brook, but in its case the planners in the 1950s-1970s failed to appreciate the benefits of retaining a continuous brook-side walk, although the mill fields to the north of the village survive. The Friends of the Wom Brook have achieved great things by giving their time and energy to regularly clear litter and wooden debris brought down by flood; by rebuilding eroded banks and by repairing/laying pathways; by removing Indian balsam; and by tree planting. Working with South Staffordshire District Council and Staffordshire Wildlife Trust they have ensured that the Wom Brook Walk is a flagship site. It has won Green Flag awards and been featured on national TV. Whilst Len Elliot of Wodehouse Farm could report in 1966 that pollution had killed the kingfishers, this is no longer true. The presence of kingfishers, dippers, herons and grey wagtails now evidence the water quality. A good array of birds can be seen along the walk, including green woodpeckers and redstarts. In 2010 a little egret was the star of the one and a half mile park. Peacock butterflies and long-eared bats can be seen in the breeding season. My aunt wrote to me in the early 2000s to say the 'water voles are back'. The otter is also back. They have been seen as far up the brook as the Wodehouse mill pool (22), probably attracted by the trout which now thrive in the stream. Otter sprait has been found from Smestow Bridge back to Wombourne itself. The support of Carillion, through its National Habitats Fund, has done much to assist the return of both water vole and otter.

Wombourne gets its name from the Wom Brook, a *winding stream in a hollow*. In 1086 Wombourne was listed as having two mills worth forty shillings. Their sites may be those associated with Mill Lane and Millhouse Farm on the Wom Brook, although there could have been a mill on the Smestow, in what was a larger Wombourne. The mill at the bottom of Mill Lane benefitted from additional water brought down by the Smallbrook. There is evidence to show its existence in 1483, 1664 and 1758, when it was a blade and a corn mill. By 1816 it was only a blade mill (23) and was occupied by Daniel Fieldhouse (24). In 1854 the mill and its cottages were advertised as Wombourne Mill, and offered for sale in three lots. Lot one included three cottages, a workshop, and the blade mill. This had an overshot wheel. Lot 2 offered two cottages, adjacent to Lot 1, for sale; whilst Lot 3 offered garden land near to Lot 1 (25). The mill pool dam provided a convenient footpath from Mill Lane to Rookery Lane (Road) and was known as the Floodgates. The buildings finished their working life in the occupancy of T Meredith, scythe manufacturer (26). In 1851 T Meredith, who was living at Orchard House (later called the Manor House), employed thirteen men in his business (27). The 1903 25-inch OS map shows that the pool had already been drained. The 1889 6-inch survey marked the pool, but no mill. The footpath across the former dam is now known as the Pool Dam.

The Wom Brook has already worked hard by the time it has reached Lower End, where Rookery Lane meets Green Hill, Gravel Hill and Common Road. In the meadow to the west of the bridge

Fig. 50   The Floodgates / Pool Dam

is the site of Ham Mill, which may have been the other one mentioned in Domesday. It was a corn mill. There is some discussion as to whether this site housed a hammer mill during the Civil War, or whether the blade mill at Mill Lane was the location. The name for the meadow is Ham Meadow. It is likely that it got its name from the Saxon word 'hamm', which means a meadow beside a stream, rather than from 'hammer mill' (28). Ham Mill is shown on a variety of Staffordshire maps – Greenwood 1820; Henry Teesdale 1831; the first edition of the OS 1 inch:1 mile of 1834. George Prior was the miller there in 1835 and he was still there in 1860. George also held the posts of registrar, parish clerk and organist, so it is not surprising that we find the Croydons, his relatives, also listed as millers in this period (29). The mill ceased production sometime during the next quarter of a century (30).

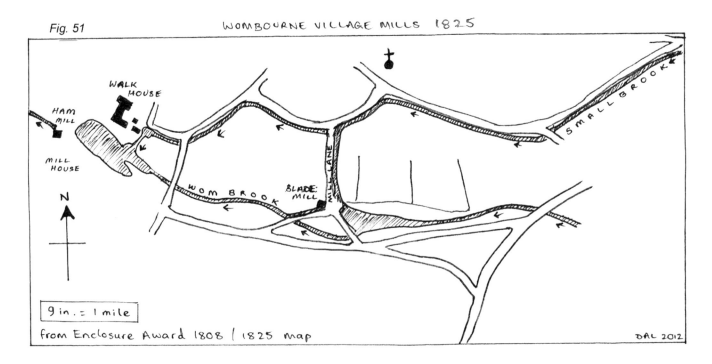

Fig. 51

Continuing its journey the Wom Brook passes underneath the trackbed of the South Staffs Railway Walk, before reaching Planks Lane. At Giggetty Bridge the canal is carried over the Wom Brook. It emerges and after a few yards flows across Dickies or Longford. A footbridge allows the walker to cross dry-shod. As an eight year old cyclist, showing how fast I could ride, my front wheels left the bridge and I and bike ended up in the ford. Despite this soaking I believe this water splash is a feature worthy of retention, as so many have been lost from the English countryside. The Wom Brook Walk continues across the Poolhouse Estate, providing an attractive setting for residents. The history of this section is dealt with in the chapter on the Smestow between Trysull and Smestow Bridge, as it includes the many leats to Heathmill pond.

Fig. 52   Longford or Dickie's Ford

The little Penn/Wom Brook has in its time powered up to six mills/forges and been an integral part of the early economy of Wombourne and Penn Common. Its role has changed and it now provides a much needed open space and a wildlife corridor, as well as adding much scenic quality to the township. For once the planners got it right.

(1)   Information from Mr John Phillips, The Wombourne Wodehouse.
(2)   Penn and Ink. Angus Dunphy 1992, P112.
(3)   Domesday Book of Staffordshire 1976. Phillimore. General Editor John Morris.
(4)   1797 John Adams map. William Salt Library.
(5)   ibid 1.
(6)   Penn Parish Register 1570-1754, Staffs Parish Register society 1921. Notes Piv.
(7)   ibid 1.
(8)   Victoria County History Volume XX. P212.
(9)   Watermills in South Staffordshire, Part 5 Smestow Brook, 1986. Cooksey, SM, and Cooksey MV. P21.
(10)   Wolverhampton Chronicle 27th April 1814.
(11)   ibid 8.
(12)   Technical drawing of Wodehouse Mill by Wilfred Foreman, 1984.
(13)   ibid 11.
(14)   The Wolverhampton Magazine August 1966. Article by Diane Maxfield P19.
(15)   ibid 8 and 11.
(16)   ibid 1.
(17)   Kelly Directory of Staffordshire 1912 and 1916 and White's Gazetteer of Staffordshire 1851.
(18)   ibid 1.
(19)   VCH Vol XX, P203-4; various editions of Wombourne Parish News and subsequently Grapevine 1981- 2011; Staffordshire Historical Collections (SHC) 1928. Ancient Deeds preserved at the Wodehouse, edited by Gerald Mander.
(20)   SHC, 1928. Deeds preserved at the Wodehouse, P25, document no. 31.
(21)   ibid 8.
(22)   ibid 1
(23)   ibid 7.
(24)   Historical Metallurgy Vol 41 pt 2. The North Worcestershire Scythe Industry, P146. Peter W King.
(25)   Wolverhampton Chronicle April 12 1854.
(26)   ibid 17. P79 and Wombourne What Was. May Griffiths 1990, P61. Uralia Press.
(27)   1851 Census. Reference to the Manor House supplied by May Griffiths.
(28)   Around Pattingham and Wombourne in Old Photographs. May Griffiths and others, 1992. Alan Sutton Publishing. P76. Additional information from May Griffiths.
(29)   Whites Gazetteer of 1834 lists John Croydon as a miller in Wombourne; and the 1851 Gazetteer lists Daniel Croydon as a Wombourne miller and it lists George Prior's jobs. Daniel is also mentioned in the tythe survey of 1851 as a brother in law to George.
(30)   ibid 8, P20.

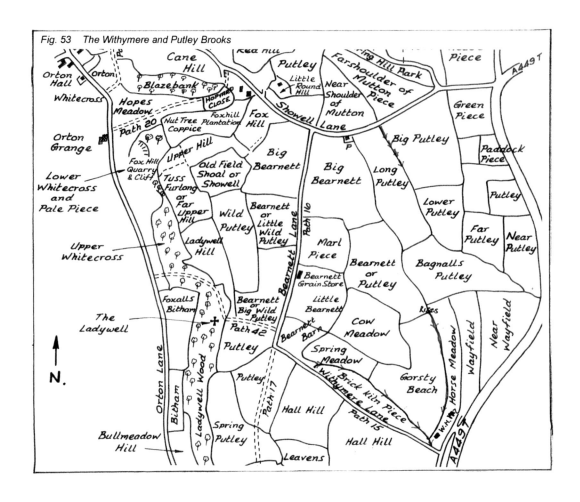

Fig. 53   The Withymere and Putley Brooks

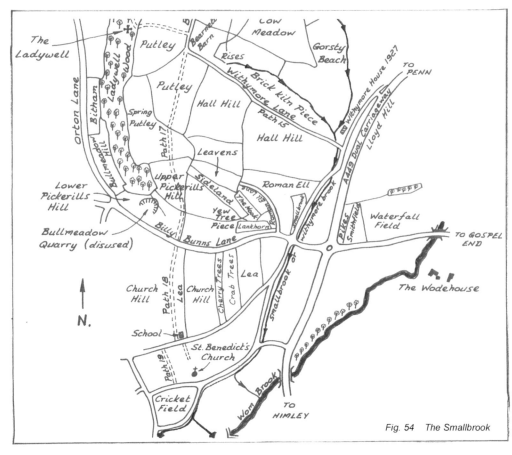

Fig. 54   The Smallbrook

82

The dip slope of the Orton Hills is home to several rivulets, whose waters surprisingly once assisted in the turning of two of Wombourne's waterwheels. The drainage basin is that of the Smallbrook, the name chosen referring to the limited volume of water carried. However, the name is not new, for Wombourne people have used it for at least seven hundred years. The Smallbrook has provided a visible sign and irrefutable evidence in deciding land ownership, as is shown in a charter of 1416, when *'John Taylor of Trysull and Andrew Jowkes of Enville granted to William Hawkys of Wombourne, three butts of land in Penn, which extended from a stream called 'Smalbroke' at the Lloyd. They formerly belonged to Thomas at Lloyd and Roger at Lloyd'* (1).

The headwaters of the Smallbrook drain the districts of Putley and Withymere. Travelling up Showell Lane from the A449T at Lloyd Hill the first of the lane's two crests is quickly reached. This is at the junction with Springhill Park (note the descriptive name), which continues to rise in a northerly direction. The lane between houses numbered 23 and 29 maintains its height, before dropping fifty feet. Several springs still weep their water in this next section. When the deep sewer was extended to this lower part of Showell Lane in 1990, the contractors found great difficulty in stemming the flow from springs and de-watering equipment had to be brought in. A low point is reached around house number 51. In the nineteenth century a cartway, which followed the

Fig. 55   De-watering operations, Showell Lane, 1990

field boundary, ran south from here back onto Lloyd Hill. However, Showell Lane continues its ascent to the scarp face of the Orton Hills. In nearby Bearnett Lane a trig point marks 550 feet.

Water from the low point in Showell Lane runs via a drain into the fields beyond. The boundary between Big and Long Putley fields has an intermittent watercourse beneath its hedge. We can call this the Putley rivulet, for want of a better name. Sandy bottomed, it is usually dry, but rain in the lane finds its way to replenish the meagre trickle. It flows laterally for a few hundred yards before vanishing, only to rise to the surface again at the field boundary between Putley, Gorsty Beach (Britch) and Horse Meadow (see map). The name Putley means a narrow neck of land joining two larger wholes. The district of Putley joined the main body of Lower Penn parish with the Lloyd, in the days before boundary changes gave these lands to Wombourne. Stronger, the rivulet now cuts down to the field boundary behind the last dozen houses at the southern end of the Stourbridge Road. It is hidden in a ditch. In early summer the growth is luxuriant. As a boy, I once, and only once, found a quail's nest here, with its ten blotchy buff-coloured eggs. Pheasant's nests were common and partridges could be seen, but finding the nest of a quail was a real privilege. A surprising and damaging occurrence is that this little brook can overflow out of its deep ditch. This occurs but rarely, the last occasion being in August 2002, when adjacent homes were flooded. The previous catastrophe happened in the late 1960s/early 1970s. The cause was incessant rain over a prolonged period and cloudburst.

The matter was made worse by the swollen waters of the Withymere arm of the Smallbrook, which rises at Joan's Well, high up on the hills at the top of Withymere, or Withymore, Lane. The latest OS maps foolishly call the lane Bearnett, ignoring centuries of local practice. Bearnett Lane is of course the lane connecting Withymere with Showell Lane. Once an eighteenth-century labourer's cottage used the supply from Joan's Well, but the cottage is long gone. The brook's gradient is steep, causing it to babble down the dip slope of the hill.

Many of the early medieval charters at the Wodehouse refer to the Caldewalle family, who are witnesses to various land exchanges in the Wodehouse/Lloyd area, and therefore play an important part in agreeing local land holdings (2). The Victoria County History refers to a Caldewell Mill in Orton in 1362 (3). Where was it? It certainly was not at the Ladywell high up in the woods on the scarp face of the Orton Hills. It is likely to have been at Orton hamlet near to Orton Hall. It could have been just north of the Wombourne station site, where the brook from Showell Bank meets the Tene Brook from Lower Penn. This location would have provided a better flow of water to service an early mill, which would have been a very rudimentary affair. An outside chance might have placed it below Joan's Well at Withymere, which lay just inside Orton liberty. Who knows?

The Putley and Withymere Brooks meet at Withymere House, a 1927 construction, much altered and added to. They then pass into the meadow, whose willow trees give the district its name. It was a favourite spot in the 1950s for gentlemen of the road to boil up a billy can over a fire of twigs, or to roast a rabbit caught in a snare further up the hill. A few yards away the drone of the traffic sweeping up Lloyd Hill provides a contrast with the tranquillity of this spot. There is time to lie back, with the turf for a pillow, and listen to the nesting birds in the willows, whilst watching the clouds billow across the sky. The withies are cut back periodically, but once they must have been harvested for basket-making and for the making of fencing hurdles. In the nineteenth century there were itinerant gipsy basket weavers at Orton, who may well have found this meadow a useful source. The sandy Hall Hill field rises from the meadow. On the bluff is a sandy hollow, which in really wet periods can sometimes partly fill with a few inches of water and upon which duck can sometimes be seen. The hollow, which is dry for most of the year, was in the eighteenth century the site for an important building, which has given us the field name. It appears in a sketch of 'A view of Wombourne from Woodhill Lane' (4).

Before being culverted to cater for the modern motorist, the Withymere Brook on leaving the meadow reappeared on the far side of the tarmac section of Withymere Lane. It eventually flowed into Smallbrook Lane and was a feature of this once rural area. The Smallbrook leaves

Townsend, or Sodom, and is culverted, beneath High Street. It once flowed in its gutter and was an accepted feature of the picturesque village of Wombourne. The 25-inch OS map of 1913 shows one arm cutting across the fields by today's police station to enter the Wom Brook at point a little distance below Rushford Bridge. However, locals don't remember this. What they do remember, and what is also shown on the 1913 map, is the brook flowing past Waverley farm (police station site) on its way to Arbour Tree House, where it turned and ran down outside the shop/cottage fronts. Some remember the Smallbrook flooding the cottages beyond Waverley Farm (5). At the junction with Mill Lane some of the water ran down a gutter on the left hand side, before dropping into the mill pool. The rest continued down the High Street to Gravel Hill. Here, it passed under the road and into Walk Lane. It reappeared from a pipe in the meadow bank, originally dropping into the mill pool of Ham Mill, and after the 1880s into the brook itself. The water of the Smallbrook was available to the cottagers, who used it for a variety of purposes as it flowed by their homes.

Fig. 56   View from junction of Withymere Lane
           and old Stourbridge Road

We have lost the visual impact of the Smallbrook on the village scene and are, I think, the poorer for it. The culverting though has ensured that poor drivers don't end up in the gutter!

(1) Historical Collections for Staffordshire 1928, Ancient deeds preserved at The
     Wodehouse, p65.
(2) ibid 1 p15-30.
(3) Victoria County History Vol XX, p212.
(4) Penn, forest, field and fireside. Angus Dunphy 2008, p14.
(5) Wombourne What Was. May Griffiths, 1990, p32. Uralia Press.

Fig. 57

SMESTOW MILL c. 1930

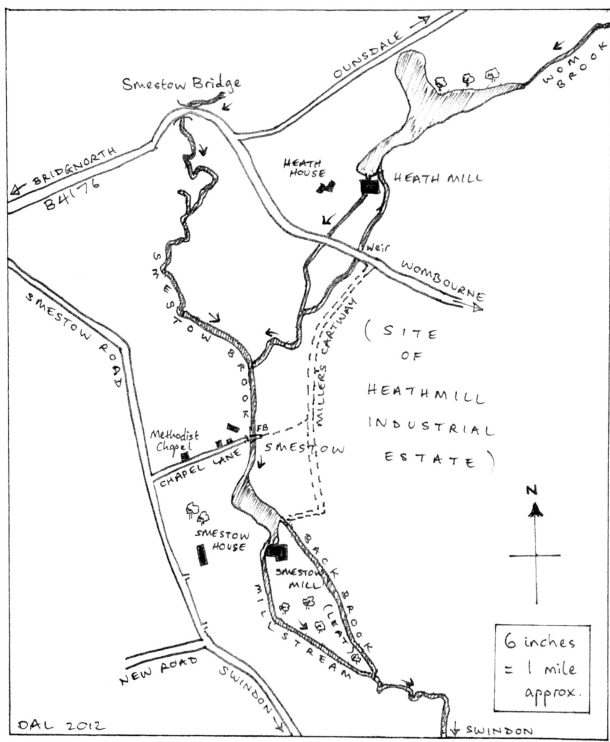

A miller's cartway (Smestow Mill Lane) still runs down to the mill from the B4176, the Bridgnorth Road (path number 39). Within this rural backwater of delights snipe once built their nests of grass-lined cups, concealing them amongst the reed beds. At dusk they rose up from the marshy valley like duck, vanishing into the murky haze of approaching night, as they sought out muddy banks upon which to feed.

Within a stone's throw the peaceful air is rent with man's noise as he works his day on Heathmill industrial estate. Built in the 1950s as part of the overspill agreement with Wolverhampton County Borough, it subsumed the fields of Smestow Mill Farm then worked by Billy Mullett.

Part way along Smestow Mill Lane is the footpath (Wombourne path 34) which crosses the valley and stream to Smestow hamlet. The footbridge was originally a couple of planks with a chain as an apology for a handrail, and known to all and sundry as Chainy Bridge. These were the days when we did not worry too much about health and safety and relied upon our own good sense to get us across.

In the war years Wombourne Civil Defence issued an A4 type pamphlet, which folded into four sections. It was called Pow-Wow ('People of Wombourne – Welding our Workers') and was meant both to inform and to raise spirits. A section was written by Jimmy Aston, the local police inspector, who had been born at the New Inn in Wombourne *(1)*. In one edition, using Black Country dialect, he told the tale of Tommy Tucker. Tommy lived at Smestow and his wife went to Wolverhampton market each Wednesday. On one occasion the weather was foul and throughout the day it got worse, until the brook was overflowing. The weather being so bad, Mrs Tucker decided to stay in town that night. Tommy was concerned, but he could do nothing until the next morning. Fearing the worst, Tommy set off to look for his wife. Squire Chinner found him at Chainy Bridge looking upstream. When asked why he was not looking downstream he replied: *"She was always awkward in life and I don't expect her to be different now!"*.

Smestow hamlet, which has the same name as the river, once boasted a Methodist chapel, where the Lamb family held sway and where a dozen or so worshippers served the cause until 1973. Today it is an attractive private house. Beyond Smestow the footpath leads to the Trysull-Swindon road.

The mill pond lay immediately upstream of the mill. An overflow leat or fleam took excess water on the eastern side of the low-lying valley. Today's tarmac access road (Heathmill Close) from the industrial estate to the mill crosses over the disused ditch, which has been left dry by the river authority reducing the Smestow's bed by between 4 and 6 feet. As a result flooding has not occurred.

Smestow Mill was there in 1816, but is not shown on Yates' map of 1775. The existing mill building probably dates from 1839, its gearing systems being contemporary with those at Wodehouse Mill (1840). The wheel which remains is made from quality castings, with well-

Pit wheel, main shaft and wallower

Fig. 58   Smestow Mill

designed curved paddles. It is approximately 14 feet 6 inches in diameter and over 7 feet wide and is of the breastshot type, as the fall from the millpond was not sufficient to power an overshot wheel. Inside the mill the machinery has been carefully preserved and forms a splendid backcloth in the ground-floor kitchen and in the bedrooms above. A broken pit wheel is placed at a right angle against the cast wallower, which encloses the main shaft. The cogging of these two wheels, when in motion, would have turned the main shaft and thus the wooden spur wheel, which is now a feature at ceiling height. The spur wheel would have cogged onto stone nuts, whose own shaft drove the grinding stones on the floor above. A crown wheel towards the top of the main shaft would have driven the hoist mechanisms. In the kitchen are four cast iron rods, which are as high as the ceiling. By moving a wooden attachment up or down, the millstones could be individually started or stopped.

Smestow Mill is four storeys high, the cable hoist remaining in the outer wall by which sacks of grain were lifted onto the third or top floor. As required they would have been lowered to the second floor and tipped into the bins. These fed four working feeds down to the four sets of stones situated on the first floor and driven from the cogged stone nuts linked to the spur wheel below. On the first storey the flour was bagged, a hatchway in the floor allowing the sacks to be lowered into the waiting carts beneath. The cartway arch can still be seen in the northern part of the building.

E and R Pratt were the millers here up until the late nineteenth century. Jasper Chinner owned it at one time. By the 1930s it was operated by Billy Mullett, until it is believed a flood damaged its wheels.

A footpath leads from the mill to the Swindon Road (Wombourne path 0.28b and Swindon path 0.78), passing the site of Smestow Hall, the home of William and Mary Chinner. They raised three sons, William, Charlton and Jasper, all born in the late 1860s. William in his youth was banished to America for some long forgotten misdeed; Charlton became a clergyman, and Jasper was renowned for his excessive spending habits. Jasper was very fond of the licensee's daughter at the Boat Inn at Botterham, now Botterham House. He courted her for forty years until her death. He regularly walked the country footpath from the mill to Botterham. It is still in use but is no longer the country walk it once was as it strikes off the industrial estate (Wombourne path number 38). Jasper drank and gambled away the family fortune, which included the Millhouse Farm and Mill at Smestow, Wombourne's Millhouse Farm, The Walk House Farm, The Foxhills, Greenhill House and several cottages at Smestow and shops at Dudley. When the fortune had gone Jasper was taken in, penniless, by the Holfords of Botterham House. He died in 1937 (2).

There is a 1920s watercolour painting of Smestow Mill looking down the valley from the Chapel Lane area. It was painted by Charles William Taylor ARCA, RE, a Sussex artist who lived from 1878-1960. At the age of seventeen he was apprenticed to a Wolverhampton firm of engravers, drawing various pieces of plumbing hardware for trade journals. There is also a wood engraving of the mill (3). An intriguing watercolour by a different artist gives a close-up view of the mill; it is painted, apparently, from a photograph of about 1900 and shows not one, but two waterwheels. The first bay or wing of the mill was where the bacon curing once took place and it is here that the wheel would have been in operation. Its exact purpose is unknown, but it may have powered a root pulper or chaff cutter or similar piece of farm machinery, as is evident at the Wodehouse Mill. However there was no evidence of a pit or machinery in 1981 when the mill was purchased by Mr Pearson. It needs to be borne in mind that the mill was derelict and falling down, with unknown persons having removed what iron they could for its scrap value.

Mr Pearson applied for planning permission in 1982 to turn the derelict mill and adjoining lands into a field study centre and Wildlife Park. Objections raised included the amount of car parking space available and access arrangements. Despite the difficulties it opened in March 1984 with falconry displays and animal talks, with a supporting cast of otters, foxes, beavers, coati, kinkajou, sloths, owls, hawks, snakes and spiders. Large numbers of children benefitted when their families began to visit from Easter that year. However, planning difficulties did not go away and the district lost an opportunity to enrich youngsters' understanding of their environment. Mr Pearson has fortunately continued with his lecture and demonstration service, which can be booked by contacting him at the mill office *(4)*. Smestow Mill is a rare gem in this modern age, and we owe Mr Pearson a debt of gratitude for his preservation and labour of love.

Beyond Smestow Mill the river flows in a south-easterly direction towards the canal at Botterham and hence to Marsh lock and Swindon village. The banks are clothed in Indian balsam and yellow flags.

(1)   POW-WOW pamphlet 1943-4. Wombourne Civil Defence, The support of Mrs Griffiths is acknowledged.

(2)   The Blackcountry Bugle, 19th November 1988. P27.

(3)   Sussex Life February 1998, and Findon Village website.

(4)   Planning and Development Committee report, South Staffordshire District Council. 21st September 1982.

Fig. 59

SMESTOW MILL TO HINKSFORD MILL

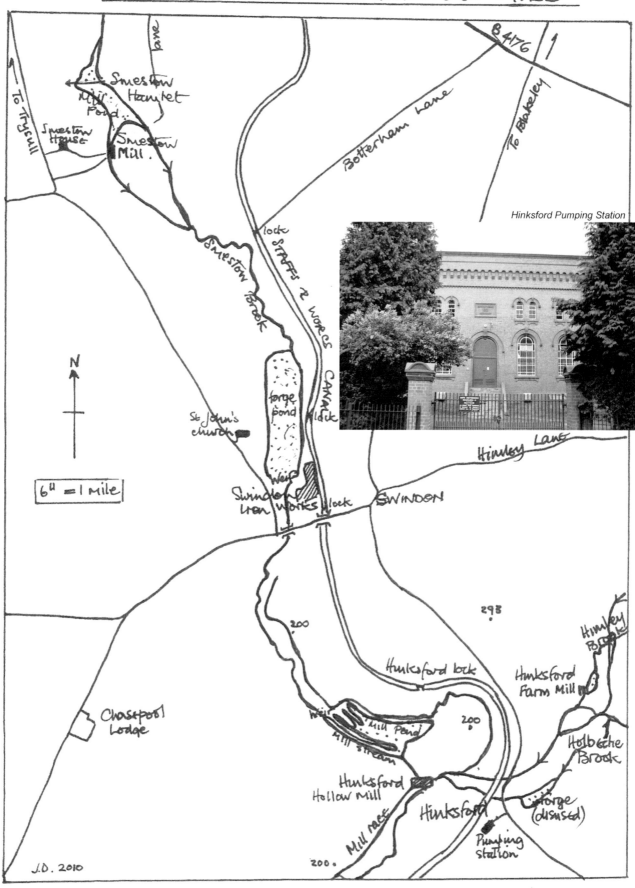

Hinksford Pumping Station

J.D. 2010

6" = 1 Mile

Shortly after Smestow Mill the canal returns to closely partner the river on its journey south. Swindon lies a short distance downstream, its past linked with its ability to harness the Smestow's power. Of particular interest in this reach of the river are the forges, blade mills and ironworks of the period 1600-1976. These were not the only users of water power, for fulling mills and corn mills were a common feature, being converted and re-converted as economic conditions demanded. In the Civil War both sides eagerly sought the weaponry of the Smestow valley's forges and blade mills.

It is likely that there was a fulling mill at Swindon in the thirteenth century (1). It passed into the ownership of Halesowen Abbey, but by the mid sixteenth century had been converted to a corn mill (2). It seems that there were still proposals to construct a fulling mill as at this time a tenter, for drying cloth, was erected (3). Dudley deeds refer to there being a watermill at Swin in 1615 (4). Quite when the forge was established is unclear. What is certain is that it was Swin Forge, and its successors, which gave the village its identity. With several others it was operated by Dud Dudley in the 1620s. The Wombourne parish register, for Swindon was then in Wombourne parish, records the tragedy that occurred at the forge in 1636 as follows:

'in this yeare happend a terrible fire at Swindon wch in the space of one houre or less, consumed and burnt downe seaven dwelling houses and other buildings to the number of 69 Bayes together with a great quantity of corne, wooll, bedding, brasse, pewter, wearing apparel, implements of husbandry and other things to the value of two thousands pounds upwards. This fire as it pleased God through sparkes flying out of Mr Lidiat's forge wch settled on the thatch of John Mathew's Barne and being carried with a great wind it was suddaine and inresistable and could not be quenched. The parties whose houses were burnt were Tho. Parkes, John Mathews, Humfrey Hilman, John Wheeler, George Tranter, William Smith, Steeven Itheridge. It hapned upon the 16th day of June about 3 of the clocke in the afternoon. The Lord sanctifie his hand to us and preserve us from the casualties' (5).

Mr Lydiat who lived at Himley could not have been a popular figure. The enormity of the fire's destruction on the lives and economy of this little village cannot be overestimated. It certainly was a flaming June afternoon to remember. Edward Lydiat sold the lease of the forge to Thomas Foley in 1645 (6). Thomas bought it outright in 1668 from Edward Jordan for £240:

'all that forge or iron mill in Swindon, mill pools and flood gate, implements, instruments, moore meadow west side of mill pool, land adjoining, two days work of land in leet fields. Right to dig turves and chark coal. To maintain waterways as has been done for last 20 years yearly rent 12d for ever' (7).

The *'two days work of land'* would have been a duty to work in the unenclosed Swindon field.

Swin and Heath Forges were worked by the Foleys in association with Greensforge. The clerk was Richard Gray. Pig iron of coldshort quality came in the main from Grange Furnace in Lower

Penn and this would have been supplemented, on occasion, by better quality pig from the Forest of Dean, transported up the Severn. Around 120 tons of bar iron was produced annually at Swin. Most went to the Hyde Slitting Mill with a little to others such as Bustleholme or Wolverley, where it was turned into rods for the domestic nail industry. Some of the bars were sold retail to Richard Ambrose and to various scythe smiths such as Wildsmith Badger or Richard Raybould (8). Philip Foley, one of Thomas's sons, took over the running of Swin Forge in 1669. He quickly sold a lease on it, believing this would bring him a bigger profit margin.

The forge passed through the hands of Clerke and Forth 1674-6. In 1674 R Davies and Joshua Rogers were paid standing wages and for mending the tools. They were given two shillings for helping get down the timber from the Orton Hill, presumably for the new helve (the wooden arm holding the heavy cast iron hammer) which was erected. A new furnace bottom was also put in (9).

Cornish, Langworth and Sergeant held Swin between 1676-8; then Wheeler and Avenant (10). In 1686 it was leased to John Podmore (a saw manufacturer of Kidderminster) for twenty-one years. By the early years of the eighteenth century William and Cornelius Hallen were tenants. They were known as frying pan makers (11).

By the 1730s Francis Homfray of Old Swinford was working Swin Forge (12). At least four generations of this family held it. It was advertised for sale in 1811 (13). Homfray and Shinton subsequently operated it until about 1820. Production was still on a small scale, although its canal-side location gave it certain advantages. In the 1830s the Thorneycrofts, Wolverhampton ironmasters, were at Swin (14). George was later to become Wolverhampton's first mayor in 1848. Bar iron and iron rods were made here at this time, but competition from larger and more productive plants on the coalfield, with their ease of supply of raw materials, posed a real threat to its survival. The never-ending list of operators of Swin reflects this view. Eli Richards, Joshua Shaw and Richard Brown were here in the 1850s; J Watkins took it in 1859 and William Watkins and Company from 1862. It was this company that gave it life, installing new equipment and extending the works with 12 puddling furnaces (process for making wrought iron) and 4 rolling mills (shaping the iron by means of rollers) (15). Coke had replaced charcoal as the fuel.

The number of ironworkers rose from an all time low in 1841 of two forgemen, one roller and one furnaceman living in Swindon, to 48 living in the parish of Wombourne. Of these 32 were puddlers, the rest being rollers, shinglers (men who hammered the puddled bar to expel the surplus slag), and forgemen. Most of the workmen lived in either Blakeley or Smestow (16).

In 1866 EP and W Baldwin leased the works, invested in it and purchased it in 1899 (17). The number employed continued to increase. Stanley Baldwin, Prime Minister on several occasions between 1923 and 1937, was Company Secretary of the family firm. He knew Swindon well and is remembered in Baldwin Way and Stanley Drive. The firm specialised in tinned and lead-coated sheets with a high percentage of tin in the coating.

After the merger of Richard Thomas and Baldwin, Swindon steelworks concentrated on hot rolling of silicon steel sheets for the electrical engineering industry, later specialising in making heavily coated tinned and terned (thin steel sheet, hot dip coated with a lead-tin alloy) sheets, which were resistant to corrosion. Closure came in 1976 as a result of a downturn in British steelworking and a rationalisation of plants.

Fig. 60   Ironworks, Swindon

Over thirty years on, and the clanging, hammering and bashing heartbeat of the village is no more. There is no towering chimney stack, shed or workshop and no busy canal wharf. What does remain is the works canteen, refurbished and operating as the community centre to this commuter village. The memories of older residents also remain to remind us of the village's contribution to the early iron industry in the West Midlands.

As the Smestow River approached Swindon it was diverted into a large pool, which ensured that the forge and later the iron works had an ample water supply. Ted Lindley remembered his boyhood in the early 1920s when he wrote that:

'moorhens and coots were a common feature of the pool, building their nests on floating reed beds. Majestic limes stood sentinel along the dam and were home to goldfinches, whilst across the brook nightjars nested in the low pollarded willows of Botterham osier beds. Kingfishers flashed their rainbow colours and trout leapt in the river, until the water was poisoned by the effluent from Courtaulds' new factory in Wolverhampton. In the nearby marshy lands, at the bank's edge wild orchids blossomed in profusion' (18).

Away from the brook, on the western bluff, is St John's Church which was built in 1854. The first burial was on 23rd July when Elizabeth Reynolds of nearby Hinksford was laid to rest, aged 101 years. She had lived through five reigns and seen Britain, through its early industrialisation, become the world's great power. The village was still small in those days, clustered around the ironworks and the crossing point on the Smestow. The workers' thirsts were quenched at three hostelries, the Green Man, the Old Bush and the Greyhound. Then there was the 1820 Congregational Chapel, a satellite of Queen St, Wolverhampton. There was also the cricket club, which today, surprisingly for a Staffordshire village, is affiliated to the Worcestershire Cricket Federation.

95

Few know of Swindon's Roman marching camp set astride the road to Highgate Common. It lies beneath Whitehouse Plantation, below the shelf along which passed the road to Uxacona (Oakengates). In the village's more recent past two tragic events were acted out. The first occurred in 1807, when William Hawkeswood, a coachman in the employ of Mr Parker of Chasepool Lodge, was convicted of poisoning his master. He paid the ultimate price. One has more sympathy for the rick burners of 1831, who set fire to farmer Richard Powell Williams' barley ricks. They feared that their employer would follow Mr Banton of Seisdon's lead, and introduce a steam driven threshing machine, thus reducing the need to hire so many agricultural workers. Tom Lloyd and John Swatkins were hanged at Stafford.

The Smestow and the Staffs & Worcs Canal leave the village as they joined it, cheek by jowl, on their journey south. The canal falls some 20 feet at Botterham double lock as it re-enters the valley. It falls a further 17 feet through Marsh and Swindon locks. The Smestow will fall another 11 feet by the time it reaches nearby Hinksford.

All rivers are downcutting their beds on their journey to reach the sea. However, the narrow valley between Swindon and Hinksford has been created by glacial meltwater. It has created the heights of Swindon Rough by scouring the western cliff, whilst depositing sands and gravels on the eastern bunter pebble bed ridge. These deposits stretch right down to Wall Heath and have been worked in places, such as along Hinksford Lane, in the north and south quarries. After the gravels have been extracted the workings are usually filled with waste and the land reinstated.

Another feature of the Swindon-Hinksford landscape, until the 1980s, was the Dudley sewage outlet pipe and sewage tanks along Hinksford Lane. In the 1870s an Act of Parliament gave Dudley Corporation the right to dump its effluent on the fields of Hinksford. The pipe ran via Gornalwood and Himley. The act was repealed at the request of Severn-Trent Water Authority in 1980 and subsequently Dudley's sewage was fed through a proper processing plant.

Below Swindon a two-room cave dwelling, with its own spring, has been carved in the sandstone cliff of Swindon Rough. The rock house was later used by John Mason, who tramped the countryside in the 1940s and 1950s, of whom more is mentioned in chapter 18.

The Smestow was again directly used to fill a large mill pond, this time north of Hollow Mill Farm, Hinksford. The leat took the excess water and formed the eastern arm of the river. A significant cutting, approximately thirty feet in height, was made in the sandstone bluff to allow the mill pool stream to power the mill machinery. It seems likely that the farm got its name from its position in the hollow.

Hollow Mill may be the blade mill at Greensforge mentioned in 1657 (19). The mill is recorded in 1678 when the watercourse leading to it was leased or re-leased, thus giving a possible date of mid seventeenth century for the cutting of the channel through the sandstone. Edward Tonge was the owner and Edward Webb of Kingswinford the

Fig. 61   Entrance to two-room rock dwelling, Swindon Rough

occupier *(20)*. Forty years later it was being used to grind timber and dye stuffs by John Crowley, son of Ambrose, a chapman from Stourbridge *(21)*. In 1720 it was advertised for sale. King suggests that it may well have reverted to a blade mill as Richard Woolley, a scythe grinder had his address there in 1751 *(22)*. In the late 1770s it was converted into a forge, probably by Francis Homfray, and became known as Swindon Lower Forge. He was succeeded by

Fig. 62   Cutting to Hollow Mill

William Finch, who offered it for sale with Heath Forge in 1793. The land tax names James Perry as tenant. It was advertised for sale again in 1798. George Briscoe held it until 1812; Mrs Briscoe until 1815 and Richard Griffiths afterwards *(23)*. It passed to James Beddard, who probably converted it back to a corn mill. In 1834 Benjamin and James Beddard were millers here and James was still here in 1851 *(24)*. Local maps suggest that the Hollow Mill had fallen out of use in the first quarter of the twentieth century and subsequently the mill was knocked down, Simpkiss, a local brewery company becoming the new owners. Jim Abbiss was the farmer. The attractive three-arch bridge over the Smestow is no longer in use and is in a dangerous state of disrepair. It has been replaced by a flat concrete structure, which provides access to the modern dwelling on the farmhouse site.

Hollow Mill Farm was the setting for an imaginary tale concerning the Gunpowder Plot of 1605. The miller's daughter had fallen in love with Catesby's servant, but as in all tales, *'all's well that ends well'*. The story entitled 'Hinksford Mill', was published in the Christmas edition of the Brierley Hill Advertiser for 1898 *(25)*.

Fig. 63   Redundant Smestow bridge, Hollow Mill Farm

Coming in from the east and passing underneath both Hinksford Lane and the canal are the waters of two additional brooks. Near here, in 1969, excavations for a gas pipeline revealed an antler artefact, dating from about 500 AD *(26)*. The Himley and Holbeche (or Holbeach) Brooks have joined forces just below Hinksford Mill Farm. This is a separate farm from Hollow Mill and is not to be confused with its neighbour. According to Dr King, a mill existed here in 1593 and was leased to Thomas Compson and his two cousins for their lifetime. He says that in 1699 it was held by Michael Raybould, a Kingswinford scythe smith, but was later let for conversion to a corn mill *(27)*. The mill is shown on William Yates' map of 1775. It stood on the high shelf above the valley of the

Fig. 64 (above and right)
Redeveloped Hinksford Mill Farm
above Holbeche Brook valley

Fig. 65 (left)
Remains of typical Smestow-system
brick arched bridge, below
Hinksford Mill Farm

Holbeche Brook and this allowed for a three-storey structure and an overshot wheel. It was fed by a long slender mill pond, since filled in. John Longville was miller here in 1851 *(28)*, and Edwin Elcock in 1868 *(29)*. The farm and mill were sold at the break-up of the Dudley Estates in 1947. Mr Cyril Whitehouse is the landowner and ex farmer. The mill house was sold, extended and much altered and little remains to remind us of its former use. The mill probably ceased working in the 1920s.

A footpath passes the mill and drops into the water meadow, where it joins the path from Hinksford to Wall Heath. It is clear to the walker that a (forge) pool once existed just above Hinksford Mill Cottage, which fronts onto Hinksford Lane. Parts of the cottage date back to at least the late seventeenth century and a

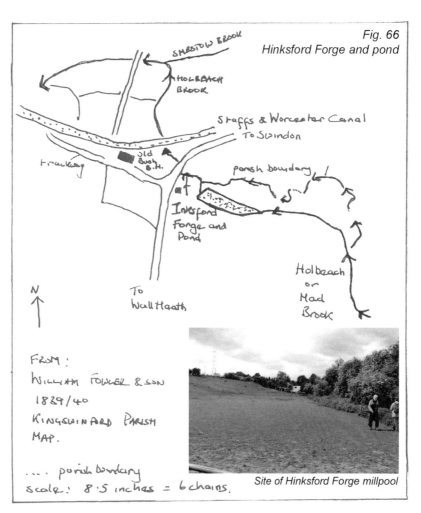

Fig. 66
Hinksford Forge and pond

Site of Hinksford Forge millpool

previous owner claimed to 1400 *(30)*. We owe a debt of gratitude to Dr King for plotting this forge's history. He says that a blade mill occupied by Griffis Eavans was amongst property leased by Edward Lyddyatt to George Bague in 1637. He goes on to recount that Nehemiah Bague acquired the copyhold in 1678 and that he sold it to Philip Foley in 1683 *(31)*. He believes that Francis Patchett, later a tenant at Greensforge, was the occupier at this point; and that he was followed by the Dancers between 1685-1705; and Jabez Bayley in 1735. He notes that by 1806 Thomas Price the Younger was using it as a forge for plating scythes and that it later passed first to Joseph Robinson and later to CF Hewitt, both of Wall Heath Forge *(32)*. The forge had ceased operations by the 1880s *(33)*.

Fig. 67
Original Old Bush pub, Hinksford – 'Cock of the Hole'

Opposite Hinksford Mill Cottage is the Old Bush, a 1930s roadhouse, which replaced an earlier beer house. This stood alongside the canal and was sometimes known as the 'Cock of the Hole', referring to its position in the hollow. Its first publican was Richard Evans in 1820, when it was open from 4am to 10pm, seven days a week. John Dutton, however, was its most famous licensed victualler. He died on 20th August 1910, aged 95 and was reputed to be Britain's oldest serving licensee. He was a Kinver man, born in Shoe Lane. After his death the family sold the pub to Joseph Paskin Simpkiss for £1025 (34).

Adjacent to the Old Bush and alongside the canal is the South Staffordshire Company's waterworks. It was built on the site of three cottages, on land purchased from John Dutton, owner of the Bush Inn. John received £100 as well as a free supply of water, not exceeding 100 gallons a day. The contractor was Henry Lovatt of Wolverhampton. He began building in 1898, facing the building with red terracotta bricks. It is one of several that tap the bunter sandstones of the Smestow Valley for their valuable supply of water and pipe it to the Black Country. However,

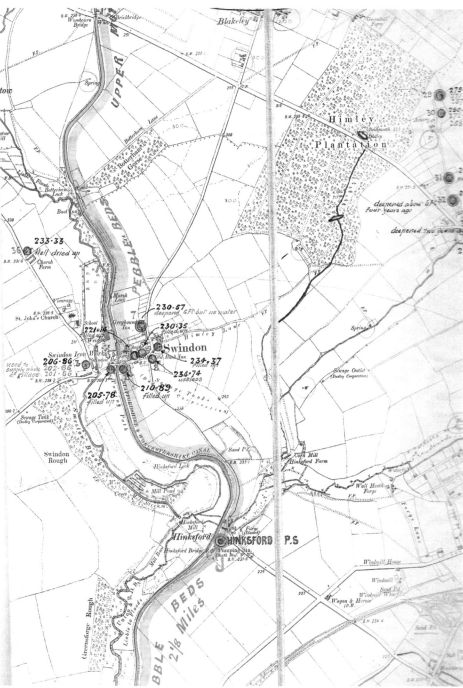

Fig. 68   Effect on village wells of Hinksford Pumping Station

drought conditions were to return to the Black Country in the summer of 1899, with many suffering from shortages. Pumping began in 1900 from a single well/bore with a depth of 272 feet. It had a considerable effect upon the villagers' wells at Swindon. Many ran dry, and had to be deepened – which still did not ensure the return of any water necessarily – or were otherwise rendered useless.

Hinksford yields up to a million gallons of water daily. The initial plant was in duplicate, made up of two inverted compound surface-condensing rotative engines, each driving a pair of bucket pumps. Electrification of the pumping plant was completed in 1950, making the canal wharf surplus to requirements (35).

The Smestow, its flow considerably swelled, meanders down to Greensforge with the heights of Greensforge Rough as its backcloth.

100

(1) Victoria County History (VCH) Volume XX, P214.

(2) Historical Collections for Staffordshire (SHC), 1928. P13.

(3) ibid 1.

(4) Information from Dr Peter King.

(5) Wombourne Parish Register, 1636. With thanks to May Griffiths for drawing it to my attention.

(6) ibid 4. Herefs RO. E12/VI/KAC/1 and E12/VI/KAC/3

(7) Dudley 6/1. Courtesy May Griffiths.

(8) Courtesy notes May Griffiths.

(9) ibid 8.

(10) RG Schafer. Genesis and Structure of the Foley "Ironworks in Partnership" of 1692. Business History 13(1), 1971, P29, 31.

(11) Herefs RO. E12/VI/KY/5 and E12/II/4/1 -references supplied by Dr King.

(12) VCH Vol XX, P213.

(13) Wolverhampton Chronicle 6 March 1811.

(14) History Gazetteer and Directory of Staffordshire, William White, 1834, P293.

(15) ibid 1.

(16) ibid 1.

(17) Ted Linley. Swindon Summer Flower Festival brochure, 1978.

(18) ibid 17.

(19) ibid 1 and reference supplied by Dr King - Dudley LHAS, D/DE/4/4.

(20) Dr PW King, Historical Metallurgy Vol 41 pt 2, The North Worcestershire Scythe Industry, P145.

(21) MW Flinn, Men of Iron, P26.

(22) ibid 20.

(23) I am indebted to Dr King for this section. Sources: Aris B'ham Gaz.18 March 1776; 12 Aug 1793; 29 Oct 1798; Staffs R.O., Land tax assessments for Wombourne.

(24) White's Directories, Wombourn entry 1834 and 1851.

(25) John Addison, Hinksford Mill, Brierley Hill Advertiser Christmas Edition 1898 and reprinted by Stan Hill, Warden at Dudley Teachers' Centre 1978.

(26) Alan V Morgan. Trans South Staffs Archaeology and Historical Soc, Vol XVII, 1975-6, Antler artefact from Hinksford.

(27) ibid 20, P145-6.

(28) ibid 24.

(29) West Staffordshire Poll Book, P154.

(30) Black Country Bugle, Hinksford Mill Cottage, Maggie James.

(31) ibid 20.

(32) ibid 20.

(33) 6" OS map.

(34) Dudley Chronicle, 20 August 1910.

(35) BV Williams and J Van Leerzem, The History of the South Staffordshire Waterworks Co. 1853-1989, chapter 3. Dudley Teachers' Centre.

Fig. 69

HIMLEY, STRAITS & HOLBEACH BROOKS
with original mill sites shown

1. Hinksford Forge / Wallheath Lower Forge
2. Hinksford Farm Mill
3. Wallheath Forge
4. Himley Mill
5. Site of Dud Dudley's Furnace
6. Oak Farm Mill
7. Coppice Mill
8. Hasco Bridge Furnace
9. Gornal Forge
10. Hunts Mill
11. Holbeche Mill
12. Cotwallend Mill

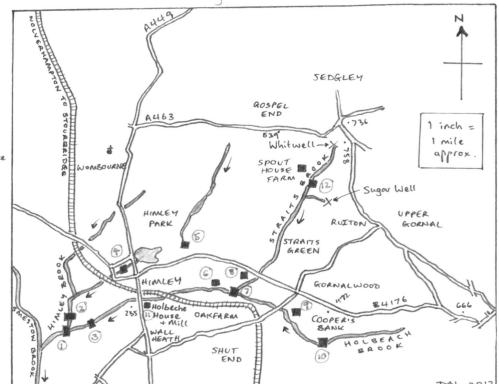

Fig. 70

HIMLEY AND HOLBECHE BROOKS – CONFLUENCE AT HINKSFORD.

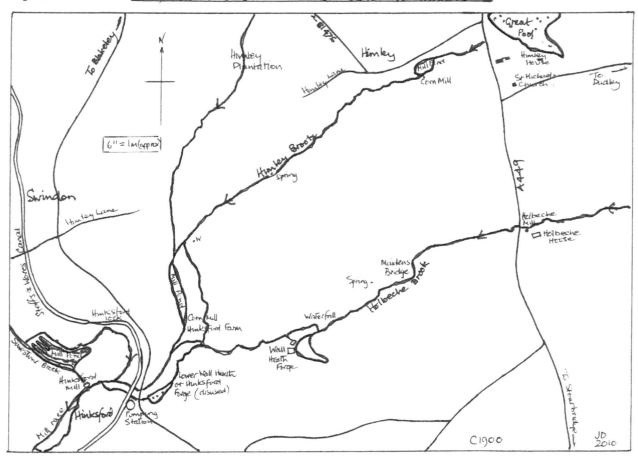

Between Sedgley and Dudley a number of streams drain the South Staffordshire plateau, falling sharply as they work their way to the Smestow at Hinksford. They provide a ready source of power, which was once harnessed to drive a succession of mills and forges.

The Himley Brook

The Himley Brook is the smallest of these streams. Its western arm begins in seepages in the gully that forms the footpath from the deer's leap in Hawkeswell Rough, where a pond once lay over the Himley Estate wall. This is on the eastern side of the A449 above Beggars Bush, Wombourne. This is the parish boundary, where in Tudor times those who had been born in Wombourne, but who were living outside the parish without visible means of support, were returned to Wombourne. Similarly vagabonds born in other parishes, but present in Wombourne, were sent on their way from Beggars Bush.

On the western side of the trunk road a rivulet gradually swells, flowing in a south-westerly direction towards Himley Plantation. The 1808 enclosure award map for Wombourne shows an upper and middle pool on respective sides of the current B4176. A third or lower pool lay north of Himley Lane. In 1998 two local men cleared out the watercourse and re-instated the lower pool. A tale, told in Rhymer Greensill's nineteenth-century ballad of Gideon Grove, was resurrected by a local newspaper in 1972: the folklore recounts that he was a servant of Stephen Littleton of Gunpowder Plot infamy, and that he was at Holbeach House on that fateful day in November 1605. He managed to get out on horseback, but was tracked by the Sheriff's men

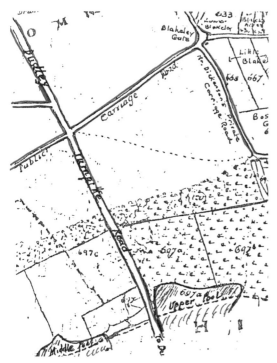

Fig. 71   1808 Enclosure Award map fpr Wombourne, and the reinstated Lower Pool, Himley Plantation

and slaughtered in a boggy area of Himley Plantation. There is of course no evidence for this, but it makes a good tale when linked with phantom riders.

Whether the water from these pools drove a mill or forge is not known. They could have simply been reservoirs for the mill at Hinksford Farm, for the brook's flow is slight.

South of Himley Lane on the road to Swindon, this arm of the brook meets the mainstream. This has started life above Baggeridge and flows via a series of lakes in a southerly direction. Viscount Dudley beautified his parkland and woods with these features. South Staffordshire District Council set up Baggeridge Country Park in 1979-80 on the former colliery site and surrounding woods. This extends over 153 acres and was opened by Princess Anne in 1983. It offers wonderful facilities for walking and joins onto Himley Park, further extending the pleasure of walking from Gospel End to Himley *(1)*.

40,000 tons of coal slurry were dredged from the Wishing Well (Whites Wood) and Spring Pools. This was left behind by one of South Staffordshire's most famous pits, Baggeridge Colliery which closed in 1967.

Aynuk and Ayli, two Black Country characters, are associated with these pools. One story tells of how they were fishing from the banks of Spring Pool when Ayli challenged Aynuk:

'I bet yo a tenna I gets a fish before yo'.

Aynuk replied, *'Yur on ar kid'.*

At that moment Ayli pulled out a whopper, but as he was wrestling with it he fell into the pool. Aynuk commented, *'that ay fur. If yo gonna dive for them the bet's orf.'*

A second story refers to the Wishing Well Pool. Ayli was courting his true love by its banks one moonlit night:

'Darlin', he says, *'con yo see that pool?'*

'Ar I con', says his sweetheart.

'Nar if that were booze an yo offered me a kiss a'hd swim in it, wi me mawth shut'.

The pools break the gradient and ensure that the stream's force is only effective over short stretches.

Beneath Spring Pool are Island Pool and the Rock Pool. Himley Hall is then reached. We know that in 1601 Lord Dudley leased Himley Hall, park and mill to Edward Stone and William Leighton for 21 years. In 1619 Lord Dudley recalled his illegitimate son, Dud, from Balliol College, Oxford to manage three of his ironworks. Dud claimed that he was successful in making iron using pit coal. In his book, *Metallum Martis,* he says that his first furnace at Cradley was swept away by the great May Day flood. He goes on to say that he made iron *'with pit cole'* at Himley Furnace. It is likely this was built upon or near to the site of the watermill. Dud met opposition from local charcoal ironmasters, who would not buy his pig iron for reworking in their forges. Himley Furnace was not a success *(2)*. In 1625 the furnace was let for ten years to Richard Foley, one of the very same charcoal ironmasters. The site of the plant is stated as being *'at or unto the Church Hall and park of Himley' (3)*.

Morton and Wanklyn note that ploughmen working in the area of the original lower pool frequently uncovered slag, which is of the same chemical composition as that produced in the seventeenth century. The furnace appears to have returned to Lord Dudley's control by 1631, the last reference to it being in 1638.

Plot published his Natural History of Staffordshire in 1686. He tells us that the whitesmith's forge made:

'sithes, reaping hooks, axes, hatchets, bills and these are ground at the blade mills to a bright edge' (4).

He says there was such a mill at Himley and another at Swindon. We can only guess at their location.

The Hall was originally a moated manor house. It was the sixth Lord Ward (and later first Viscount), John, who in the period 1740-52 set in hand the replacement of his medieval manor house, creating more or less what we see today. In 1764 St Michael's Parish Church and much of the original village were re-sited well away from the Hall to give it a finer setting. John died in 1774 and was succeeded by the second Viscount. Wishing to enhance his status, he engaged Capability (Lancelot) Brown to give the park a pastoral setting (5). The Himley Brook was made to flow in a broader channel to give the appearance of a river and the Great Pool was made, replacing the lower pool, which had been much nearer the house.

The Himley Brook exits the Great Pool via a sluice and reappears alongside the car park of the Dudley Arms Pub. It flows down through the water meadows to Himley Mill, now a private residence. A mill pond once existed which fed the mill through an internal overshot wheel of 13 feet 6 inches diameter and 5 feet 6 inches width (6). The red-brick corn mill was in operation until the twentieth century and the machinery was still in place at the time of the Great War. The Cartwright family of nearby Whitehall Farm were millers in the first half of the century and later the Leighs. Both families, who may have been related, also ran the Dudley Arms (7). Himley Mill and the mill pond were sold at the break-up of the Himley Estates in 1947. Lot 26 included a pair of roadside cottages and two cottages at the rear, together with the two- and three-storey mill buildings. The Lot sold for £1800 and was just over an acre in extent. The mill pond and adjacent garden ground of some two acres sold for £450. The mill's name has been perpetuated in the nearby nursing home. Other nineteenth century residents of Himley included the Bates family – they were millwrights and were also linked with Compton Mill.

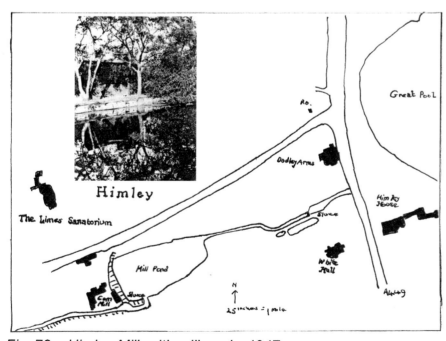

Fig. 72   Himley Mill, with millpond c.1947

Fig. 73
Himley Mill, pool dam and loading arch

Today's mill, mill house and barn are in separate ownership and all are private property. They were once held by Mr Alan Hickling. His son, Tony, first began to turn the mill into a private residence in the early 1970s. Vee and David Hingley have owned it since 1976 and have made it into an attractive home. Certain aspects remain to remind us of the activity which once engaged the miller on this site. Beneath the house are very extensive cellars, which reflect the skill of the builders in siting the property into the valley side. The brickwork on the western face provides clues as to the position of two cart bays, which existed for unloading and loading grain and flour. The extensive outer dam wall is very much in evidence to the south of the house. It is made up of massive Triassic sandstone blocks – many with a diameter of 4' x 3'6" x 3'6" – that must have been quarried on or near the site. These must also lie underneath the house extension. The adjacent patio area has been created by removing tons of puddled clay, which formed the core of the dam, whilst its inner facing was lined with smaller pieces of sandstone, which are part of today's rockery. The remains of the sluice that allowed excess water to leave the mill pond is also in evidence. Below the level of the upper garden the brook's new course can be seen. In the house's living room the cut-out portions in the beams evidence the position of the water wheel, axle, rods and pulleys which were busy working the mill stones and hoists (8).

Leaving the village, the brook flows in a south-westerly direction underneath the bypass and the old railway until it meets the stream from Himley Plantation, just north of Hinksford Mill Farm. The brook then falls into the valley of the Holbeche Brook, before reaching the Smestow at Hinksford.

The Straits Brook

The Straits Brook, also known as the Bobs (or Bob's) Brook, rises in the ridge wall of Sedgley/Ruiton. The Whitwell, one of Sedgley's early wells, lies in the fields beyond Moden Hill. From here the brook trickles down the steep slopes to Cotwallend Nature Reserve, filling its pools. Water from the spout at Spout House Farm adds to the volume. The lower pool (Whites, after White Well) was once the ancient 'Mulle Pool', recognisable as such until mid-twentieth century. Whilst no mill is mentioned in Domesday for Sedgley Manor, two are subsequently alluded to in the medieval period. One of these is thought to be that at Cotwallend (1). A drive down Cotwallend Road (previously Downings Lane and Whites Lane) gives the motorist a sense of the gradient and longitudinal profile of the brook. From the east the Dingle stream joins on an even steeper gradient. It has begun in the Sugar Well, whose sweet water supplied Ruiton in former times. The well is surrounded by its sandstone cistern, from which the water flowed to fill an ornamental pond or two in the Ellowes Park. The parkland was part of Ellowes Hall (Ellers to

Fig. 74   Cotwallend mill pool

Gornal folk), which sat up on the bank and looked out over the South Staffordshire and Shropshire countryside. The hall was built by a South Staffordshire ironmaster, John Turton Fereday in 1821. Whilst the ironmasters and the hall have not withstood the ravages of time, a secondary school retains the name and benefits from its parkland setting.

The faulted Cotwallend Valley was worked for coal by small pits and levels between the 1920s and the early 1960s. The thick coal outcropped near to the base of Turners Hill and Straits Green Colliery was once connected to the Earl of Dudley's Pensnett Railway by a tramway. In the past Turners Hill has provided Silurian limestone. The lime was burnt and spread on the fields as well as being used as a lime wash. The hill is capped with Devonian sandstone, whilst the footpath from The Ellers to the Straits is known as 'Slither Bonk', because of its Carboniferous clays and marls.

Gornal/Straits are a geologists' paradise. The yellowy Devonian sandstone seen in the buildings, walls, copings, stiles and boundary markers was also suitable for making querns – hand mills. Indeed, the word Gornal is thought to have been derived from the name. Between the Straits and Sandyfields is the site of the Red Quarry where the red Carboniferous sandstones were cut and subsequently made into grindstones. These were important for the eighteenth century's scythe industry, with many workers listed in the Sedgley parish register.

At the bottom of the Cotwallend Valley, near to Turners Hill, was a fording place of the Straits Brook. Known as Wrigglesford, the name refers to the crossing point for young sheep *(2)*.

The Bobs Brook is swelled by water from the hillside near the site of the Gornal gasworks. Here there was an osier bed with a pond. Did this once drive a mill or was it just an osier bed? The Bobs or Straits Brook is also joined by the stream from the Wallows, shortly before it reaches Askew Bridge.

The Straits Brook flows under the road of the same name and heads for Askew Bridge and the old Toll House (Pop House) on the B4176. At times of flood a pond appears beneath the embankment. This was one of two furnace ponds which drove Dud Dudley's bellows at his Hasco Bridge Furnace. The furnace site and second pond lay south of the Himley Road but mining for coal and open casting for fireclay have resulted in the loss of the site.

In his book Metallum Martis Dud writes:

'the author erected a new large Furnace, 27 feet square, all of stone for his new invention; the Bellows of which Furnace were larger than ordinary Bellows are, in which he made 7 Tons of Iron per week, the greatest quantity of Pit-cole-Iron that ever yet was made in Great Britain; near which Furnace the author discovered many new Cole-mines 10 yards thick, and Iron-mine under it, according to other Cole-works; which Cole-works being brought unto perfection, the author was by force thrown out of them and the Bellows of his new Furnace and Invention, by riotous persons and cut in pieces, to his no small prejudice.' (3)

Askew Bridge Furnace was large by normal standards and its annual production could have been thrice that of the usual furnace of the time. Dud Dudley's significance is that he greatly contributed to the knowledge then available for the smelting of iron using coal. He claims to have done it at both Himley and Askew Bridge Furnaces and to have sent samples of iron to the Tower to be tested. Morton and Wanklyn have demonstrated that Dud:

'used coal or pre-coked coal at least as part of the charge and that the larger bellows at Askew Bridge would permit higher operating temperatures and allow the use of higher lime burdens. He therefore could have succeeded in smelting iron ore with mineral coal, or coke. He would therefore be able to manufacture a range of cast products, including armament'. *(4)*

He was a man before his time. The West Midlands would have to wait another ninety years before Abraham Darby's re-invention and a further fifty years before coke-smelted pig was successfully converted to wrought bar iron. The power of these local brooks in providing sufficient heads of water cannot be over-estimated in the story of iron smelting and working.

The Straits Brook cuts down through Gornalwood Coppice before joining the Holbeche Brook on its journey to the Smestow at Hinksford. A mill pond is shown on the 1775 Yates map at the confluence of the two brooks. Beyond this lay Coppice Mill on the Holbeche Brook. It is named on the first edition of the OS 1-inch map (sheet 62) of 1834. Its site was adjacent to Askew Bridge junction on the Pensnett Railway.

The Holbeche (or Holbeach) Brook

Holbeche, or Holbeach, Brook falls the greatest distance, as the ground from the Shavers End/Eve Hill/Old Park area is at a height of seven hundred feet. Schubert states that the first blast furnace in the area, south and west of Dudley, was built at Gornalwood in 1595 (1). It was leased by '*Lord Dudley to Richard Hamnett. In 1607 Thomas Hickmans was there and John and Nicholas Guest took a lease on a former furnace pool in 1648*' *(2)*.

Quite where this furnace was is open to conjecture. Did it lie high upon the tributary stream that flowed down from Dibdale through the Graveyard (Grosvenor Road) area? Or was it subsequently the site of the later forge, which is remembered by the nearby Forge Inn in Chase Road and by Smithy Lane? Gornal Forge and forge pool was still shown on Fowler's second edition map of Kingswinford parish in 1839/40 (3). This forge was driven by the waters of the Holbeche Brook, which formed the parish boundary. Nearby was a further stretch of water, the long slender Fillwell Pool, which was filled by the Dibdale

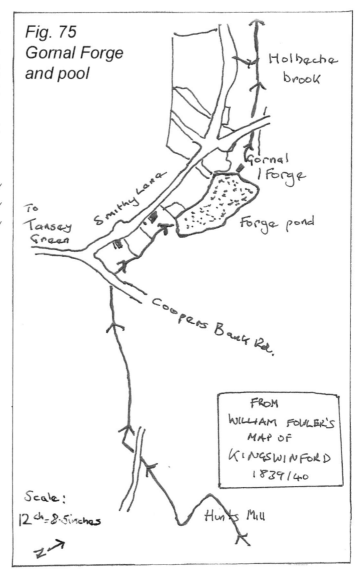

Fig. 75
Gornal Forge and pool

tributary and which lay alongside Cinder Road *(4)*. The Fillwell Pool could have been a header pond, if a leat ran back to the forge, but it may have driven its own machinery, as the confluence of the Dibdale and Holbeche Brooks lay further downstream. King points out that a furnace is mentioned as being excluded from a lease concerning Dudley Old Park *(5)*. Could therefore the 1595 furnace have been on the site of Hunts Mill at Coopers Bank or was it higher up? These questions remain until further research establishes a true picture.

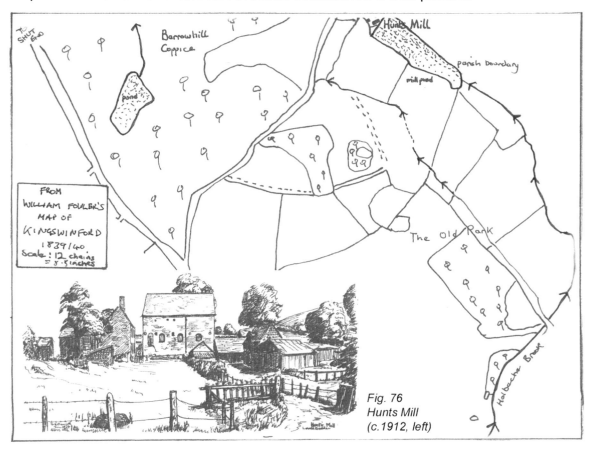

Fig. 76
Hunts Mill
(c.1912, left)

The corn mill at Hunts Mill was an impressive eighteenth-century building, which dominated the farm until its demolition in the late 1970s. Unusually the mill wheel was housed inside the building. Yates shows the site of the mill and pool on his map of 1775, as does the Ordnance Survey 1 inch to the mile map of 1834. Fowler's Kingswinford map gives greater detail of its extent. The boundary with Sedgley manor is also shown, as it passes through the mill pond and runs along the bank of the brook. The 25-inch 1903 map, however, does not show the mill pool. John Marsh Fellows and Joseph Fellows were millers both here and at Holbeche Mill in 1872 *(6)*. However as the twentieth-century directories do not give an entry for Hunts Mill, it would seem that farming in the district had largely given way to the more lucrative mining and that milling had ceased. I visited the mill once in the mid 1970s and was impressed by the sound, speed and power of the rushing water.

The patch of countryside below Hunts Mill has been worked and reworked for coal and fireclay. The district has been scarred by pit mounds and flooded marl pits, as well as by being criss-crossed with lines of the Earl of Dudley's private railway, the Pensnett. The watercourse has therefore been culverted in places, but generally it follows the trackbed of the Pensnett line to Askew Bridge Junction, west of Sandfield Bridge on Cinder Road. Beneath the sewage works and on the far side of the old rail track is an overgrown pool, once a header for Coppice Mill. After the Straits Brook has joined the Holbeche, the now considerable waters flow on through the worked-out Himley Coalfield to the Glynne Arms, or if you are from Gornal 'The Sidden House' (the Sunken House). The Crooked House, as the pub is generally known, suffered from mining subsidence in the nineteenth century. It lay at the boundary between Sir Stephen Glynne's lands and those of the Earl of Dudley. The former worked the coal up to the boundary, with the resultant drunken state that the building presents. Here you will find truth stranger than fiction, for a bottle rolls up the table and the grandfather clock stands at an amazing angle. Only the chandelier hangs true. In the 1950s Banks brewery saved this miners' and ironworkers' beer house by carrying out extensive remedial work.

Sir Stephen Glynne owned some one hundred acres at Oak Farm, the property being rich in coal, ironstone and fireclay. He refused an offer of £35,000 in 1835 and subsequently gave his agent, Mr James Boydell, free range to develop it. Boydell set up furnaces, forges and rolling mills and plant for producing tools and hardware. The capital for this expansion was raised on the Glynne fortune and on their Hawarden Castle Estate, near Chester, which ran to 7000 acres (7).

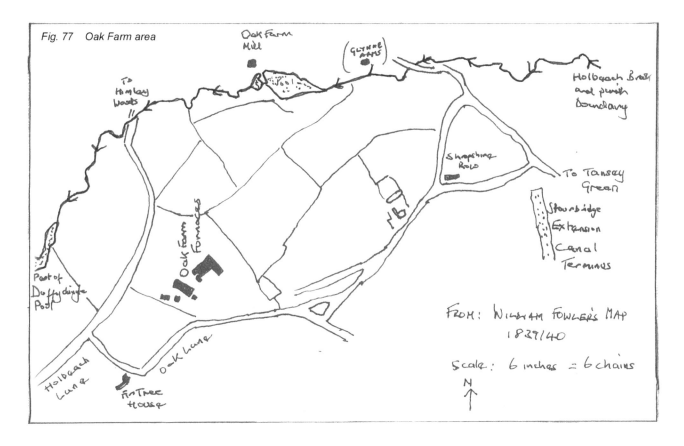

Fig. 77   Oak Farm area

The late 1840s saw the Oak Farm Company slide into insolvency. In 1847 there was an orgy of speculation on the Stock Exchange and the Company was forced into liquidation on the petition of Lord Ward, one of the creditors. Liabilities were estimated at £450,000. The bankruptcy is important in national history because William Ewart Gladstone was a brother-in-law to the Glynnes. As such he represented the joint family interests at the bankruptcy proceedings in 1848. Oak Farm was to cost Gladstone an estimated one-third of his income over the years, but it did give him valuable industrial and commercial experience as he prepared to become a future Chancellor of the Exchequer and then Prime Minister.

The Oak Farm Company's assets were auctioned off in April 1849 at the Dees Royal Hotel in Birmingham. The sale included the Glynne Arms, described as:

'that conveniently situated and commodious dwelling house, now used as a public house, with garden, outbuildings, stabling, and appurtenances and water corn mill, now in the occupation of Mr John Cartwright' (8).

It would seem that Oak Farm Mill was located at the Crooked House and not at nearby Coppice Mill. Severe flooding has occurred at the Crooked House on several occasions. One such flood in the early years of the twentieth century created a large lake outside the pub and made passage across the valley impossible *(9)*.

Beyond the Glynne Arms the Holbeche Brook flows west, once filling the now silted Daffydingle Pool (first mill pond for Holbeche Mill). This pool was cut in two by the construction of the Ashwood-Baggeridge branch of the Pensnett Railway. At Holbeche Osiers, the Kingswinford Junction to Oxley Junction Railway (GWR Stourbridge to Wolverhampton via Wombourn Line) was in course of construction in 1915. Initially the brook was culverted underneath the new railway, unsuccessfully: when severe flooding occurred, subsidence caused the embankment to slip. Rails were left suspended *(10)*. The brook descends into a narrow valley, a batch, from which Holbeche gets its name. The brook is the boundary between Himley parish and Kingswinford.

Fig. 78   GWR Holbeche Osiers north side landslip, July 1915

Stephen Pratt was the miller at Holbeche in 1834. It was still a corn mill in 1888, when David Phillips was the miller, but it probably ceased working at the time of the First World War or shortly afterwards. There was a small mill pond, immediately east of the mill. It was drained in the mid 1920s. The mill was a red brick, three-storey building with ground floor dimensions of roughly 24 feet by 17 feet. There was an external wheel driving two pairs of stones. Holbeche Mill was knocked down in the 1960s.

A site survey was carried out by Worcestershire County Council Archaeological Service in 1999 *(11)*. The dig revealed domestic shards of pottery of sixteenth and seventeenth century date, possibly suggesting that a mill may then have existed on this site. Evidence was found of two phases of corn mill, with their own head and tail races. The first mill dated from the late eighteenth/early nineteenth century, when stone was used in its construction. The later nineteenth-century mill was brick built, as was the sluice and wheel pit. A large stone wheel was found which was thought to be part of a cider press, suggesting that the mill both ground corn and produced cider in its later days.

On the southern bank is Holbeche House, famous (as mentioned earlier) for its role in the Gunpowder Plot. It was owned by Stephen Littleton, one of the plotters, and was their last refuge. On the seventh of November 1605, on their flight across the Midlands, they crossed the Stour and got their powder wet. They arrived at Holbeche at 10pm and made the mistake of trying to dry the powder in front of an open fire. It was ignited, destroying part of the house and badly burning Catesby and Rokewood. Robert Winter and Stephen Littleton deserted their fellow plotters and went to hide in the neighbouring woods. At midday on the 8th November Sir Richard Walsh, the Sheriff of Worcestershire, and his men arrived and surrounded the House. In the ensuing one-sided fight Catesby, the leader, was killed and Percy and the Wright brothers seriously injured. Morgan, Thomas Winter, Rokewood and Grant were taken.

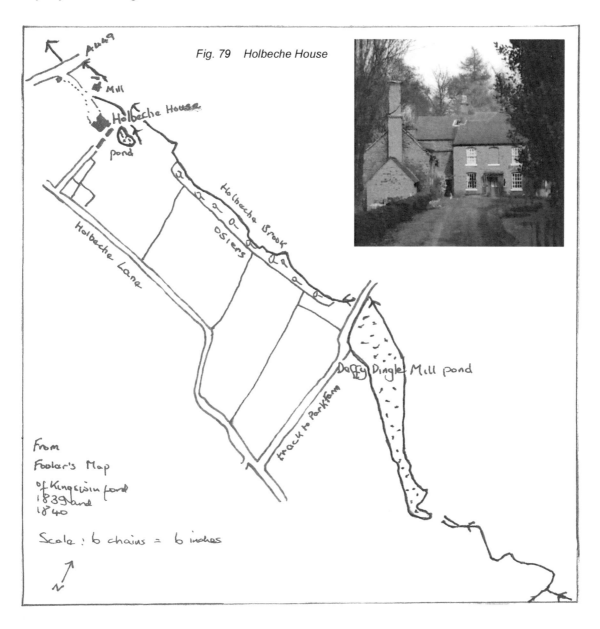

Fig. 79   Holbeche House

The brook flows on, underneath the A449 and through the meadows to Maidensbridge. Generations of Wall Heath children know it as the Mad Brook and have fished and played in it. At the north-western end of Wall Heath was the Forge and its pond. A mill is shown at this spot on Yates' 1775 map. Dr King has researched the history of the forge. He informs us that Joseph Robinson, a miller, was left the mill by his father in law, Thomas Raybould, a scythesmith. Joseph was running the mill in 1783. By 1822 it was called Wall Heath Forge and by 1834 was

113

the property of CF Hewitt. Job Legge rented it in 1856 and subsequently bought it in 1858, but he quickly disposed of it to Isaac Nash of Belbroughton. This family sold it in 1909 on the death of Isaac, the son of Isaac. The forge produced spades, shovels and edge tools *(12)*. The mill building and pool have succumbed to Dudley's need for housing.

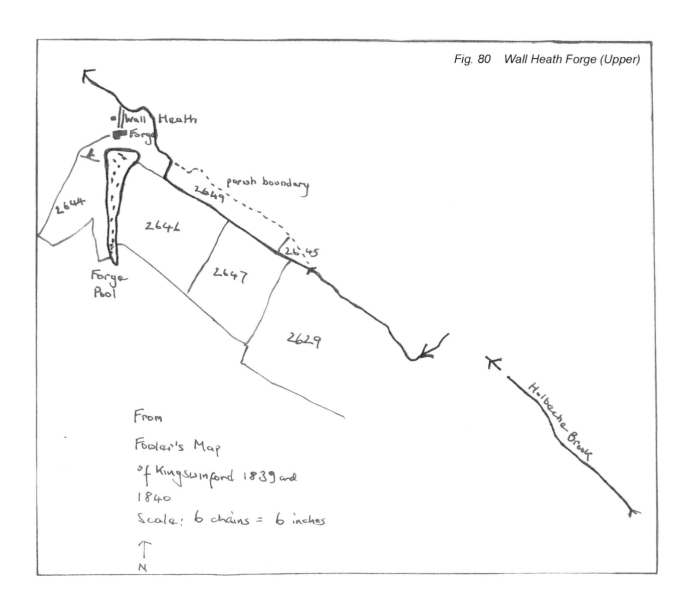

Fig. 80   Wall Heath Forge (Upper)

A public footpath leads from the site of the forge pool down to Hinksford. Walking along it a sense of the brook's power is felt as it busily tumbles its way towards the Smestow at Hinksford. The Holbeche Brook has been downcutting since the end of the last ice age, when meltwater lowered the bed of the River Severn and many of its tributaries. The Holbeche Brook, in its short journey, has fallen by some 500 feet or so.

The Himley Brook joins the Holbeche Brook shortly before the site of Wall Heath Lower Forge at Hinksford. This is marked by Hinksford Mill Cottage. The Holbeche Brook passes underneath both Hinksford Lane and the canal and reaches the Smestow.

Himley Brook

1) *Historical Notes on back of Alan Godfrey Old OS Map - Sedgley West, 1900, Sheet 67:06. Angus Dunphy.*
2) *Metallum Martis or iron made with pit coale. Dud Dudley, 1665. 1854 edition. P11-12.*
3) *Dud Dudley A New Appraisal, West Midland Studies Vol 1. GR Morton, MDG Wanklyn, 1967. The Polytechnic, Wolverhampton.*
4) *The Natural History of Staffordshire. Robert Plot, 1686. Chapter 9, P375.*
5) *Himley Hall and Park. DF Radmore, 1982. Dudley Leisure and Recreational Services. P8.*
6) *Watermills and Water-Powered Works on the River Stour Part 5: The Smestow Brook. SM Cooksley and MV Cooksley, 1986. P19.*
7) *Various directories - Parson and Bradshaw 1818; Whites 1834; Whites 1851; PO 1872.*
8) *Information gathered from a visit to Himley Mill by kind permission of Mr David and Mrs Vee Hingley.*

Straits Brook

1) *Studies in Sedgley History. FA Barnett, 1975. Dudley Teachers Centre Item 3637.*
2) *A History of Lower Gornal. FA Barnett, 1975. Dudley Teachers Centre Item 3636.*
3) *Metallum Martis. Dud Dudley, 1665. P12.*
4) *Dud Dudley A New Appraisal. GR Morton and MDG Wanklyn, 1967. P57.*

Holbeche Brook

1) *A History of British Iron and Steel. HR Schubert, 1957. RKP. P180.*
2) *Watermills and Water Powered Works on the River Stour Part 5. SM Cooksley and MV Cooksley, 1986. P19.*
3) *Fowler's Map of Kingswinford, second edition, 1839/40.*
4) *A History of Lower Gornal. FA Barnett, 1975. P8.*
5) *Correspondence with PW King, 2009.*
6) *The Post Office Directory for Staffordshire. P635, P1022.*
7) *Over and nether Penn and district. A Dunphy, 1994. P148-159.*
8) *Oak Farm Coal and Iron Works Important Sale. Wolverhampton Chronicle 4th April, 1849.*
9) *The Bugle Annual 2008, P46-7.*
10) *Oxley Junction-Kingswinford Junction Branch Line. A Dunphy, 1976. Dudley Teachers Centre Item 3760. P26-9.*
11) *Watching Brief at Holbeche House. M Cook, 1999. Archaeological Service, Worcestershire CC, Project P1583, Report 726.*
12) *The North Worcestershire scythe industry. Historical Metallurgy Vol 41 Part 2. PW King, 2007. P146.*

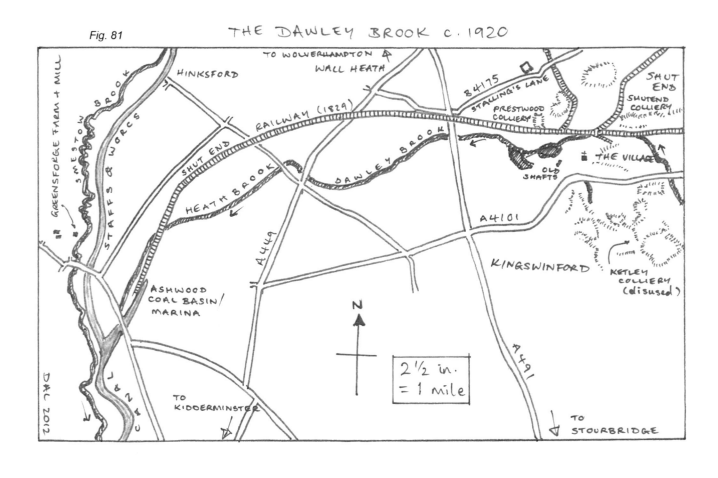

Fig. 81

THE DAWLEY BROOK c. 1920

The Dawley brook has a district of Kingswinford, an industrial estate and a primary school named after it. It rises in several places in the Ketley quarry/Corbyn's Hall areas and for much of its course is culverted across Kingswinford, before dropping down from the plateau to flow to the Smestow at Ashwood.

Ketley and Corbyn's Hall are names that are synonymous with coal mining and iron making. One hundred and seventy years ago John Gibbons was the ironmaster at Corbyn's Hall. He published *Remarks on the Puddling and Blast Furnaces (1)*, in which he explained the experiments that he carried out to maximise iron production.

John knew, like every other ironmaster, that after four or five years a blast furnace needed relining with firebrick. He examined his blown out furnace and found that changes had taken place to its square interior, in that it had become 'rounded off'. So, in building his new number 4 furnace, he constructed it with a conical interior. He then compared its production with those of his traditional furnaces. Number 4 produced 100 tons of pig iron per week, as against his more usual output of 75 tons.

What John Gibbons had done was to extend the base of the furnace upwards to about thirty feet (as against the usual twelve feet). The increased height allowed hotter temperatures to operate in the upper part of the furnace, thus causing a quicker chemical reaction, with a resulting economy in fuel consumption. His work was copied at the nearby Ketley furnace, where a weekly production of 236 tons of pig was achieved.

He also carried out experiments to the puddling process for the making of wrought iron. His technological innovations helped set the scene for others to follow and briefly helped south Staffordshire reach a pre-eminent position in the iron trade.

The Ketley and Corbyn's Hall areas were heavily mined for coal, ironstone and fireclay. Two documents dated 1842 show Benjamin and John Gibbons' plans for guaranteeing future supplies of raw materials. The first document was an agreement with Messrs Matthews and Dudley (2), whereby Matthews and Dudley agreed to surrender their lease of certain mines and to surrender pit number one by Christmas 1842 and pits 5 and 6 at Christmas 1850. In return they were to receive the Rookery pits and the pits on the Tiled House estate.

The second document reflected the valuation, by Mr Fowler, of the 111 acre Tiled House Estate at Pensnett at a massive £60,000 (3). The Kingswinford area was similarly blessed, showing us the value of what lay beneath the surface of the lands drained by the upper Dawley Brook. Ketley, Planet, Prestwood and Elm Tree are but a few of the collieries that once worked this area. However, with the pits came a despoliation of the landscape, which was not unlike a scene from the Somme. In amongst the pit head gear, winding engines and spoil banks were structures of an earlier and a healthier age. The tower of the medieval church of St Mary stood above the gloom. White writing in 1834 commented upon the interior of this church, which displayed monuments to the great local families of Corbyn, Scott, Hodgett and Bendy. But, he also made a more telling comment by saying that the church was already too small to meet the needs of a fast expanding parish and therefore a new church had been built at Wordsley, as well as a chapel of ease at Brierley Hill (4).

Near to St Mary's was the site of Bradley Hall, a half-timbered house of the late sixteenth century, demonstrating that there was a past before coal mining took hold. Unfortunately it was sold for £2775, dismantled by Messrs AH Guest and re-erected at Stratford upon Avon in 1925 (5).

Fig. 82   Bradley Hall, Kingswinford

The industrial scene of the nineteenth century was completed by the Shutt (Shut) End Railway, the West Midlands' first standard-gauge steam-hauled line. It was opened on 3rd June 1829 and linked Shut End and Kingswinford with Ashwood Basin on the Staffordshire and Worcestershire Canal. It was the 1830s equivalent of the M5 in that it allowed the export of iron and coal all the way down the Severn Valley to Bristol. The railway was built as a result of an agreement of 1827, between Lord Dudley and James Foster (of the future Shutt End ironworks). It ensured that Foster could get ample supplies of raw materials to his works from the many nearby pits. Whilst Lord Dudley and James Foster owned or controlled most of the land, there was a small patch of ground at Stallings Farm, near to St Mary's Church, which was owned by Mr Foley. A separate lease had to be negotiated. The Corbyn's Hall collieries were connected by a short length of track to the system.

On the opening day the engine, the Agenoria (named for a Roman goddess of courage and industry), pulled eight coaches carrying 360 official passengers; hundreds more took a ride that day by hanging on to the coal wagons (6). Agenoria was built by Raistrick at his Stourbridge foundry. She worked the line until 1885, and is now in the National Railway Museum at York. A half-mile connecting line was opened in 1846, allowing coke and coal to reach the district of Dawley Brook from the Himley coalfield. By joining the Shut End and Himley sections of the Earl of Dudley's Railway, the system became known as the Pensnett. The original line ran just beyond the northern edge of Kingswinford Park and eventually had a branch running back to the Planet Colliery and the A4101. From the grounds of today's Blandford Mere School the line progressed westwards, crossing the A491 near the then Bridge public house on a single-span iron girder, which for a time advertised Baggeridge Coal. When the National Coal Board ceased to send Baggeridge coal to Stourport Power Station, via this route, the line became redundant. The last train ran to Ashwood Basin in October 1953, since when the coal wharves have been turned into an extensive marina.

So this was the industrial scene through which an ever more polluted Dawley Brook flowed. Today, much cleaned up, it flows below the new housing development of Meadowsweet Way/Ploverdale Crescent on a quickly falling gradient, before passing underneath the A4101,

118

Kingswinford to Pensnett Road. It turns west skirting the Pensnett Trading Estate, before entering, via a culvert, the eastern arm of the lake in Kingswinford Park. The lake is used as a balancing pond to regulate its variable flows.

Fig. 83   Kingswinford Park lake

Another arm of the Dawley Brook is culverted underneath the A4101 from the Greenfield Road area. It flows into the private pool beneath the park lake. The Park was created from eleven acres of industrial waste land, which was sold by George Fenn and George Guest to Brierley Hill Urban District Council in 1939. The slag and pit mounds were levelled and the swags (pools created by subsidence) turned into lakes, to create a park, which was bravely opened to the public in 1940.

Fenn and Guest also sold adjacent land to John and George Holland, who subsequently transferred it into the Council's ownership in 1947 (7). This was added to the George VI Coronation Park. Mr Tom Percival, of Summerhill Grange, gave £5000 to Brierley Hill for the purchase of the land (8).

A feature of the site is its ability to flood after prolonged rain. During the last forty years much has been done to alleviate the problem and upgrade the Park and its facilities. Work started in the 1970s with dredging out and enlarging the pools. Tree planting was a feature of the Millennium activities and this not only provided a scenic backcloth, particularly in autumn, but assisted with lowering groundwater levels. Between 2003-8 the work of an active volunteer group assisted by the Council did much to improve the facilities for the local populace – pleasant open spaces for families, a games area, clearly defined paths for walkers, a performance area, a larger lake area with improved retention walls and areas for model boat club members to enjoy their leisure activity, a bandstand, and a club house for the bowling club. However, in June 2007 an exceptional rainfall of 5.5 inches falling in just eighteen hours flooded the Park (9). The Dawley Brook broke its banks, flooding the industrial estate of the same name as well as private residences and shops.

The brook, flowing in an open channel, partners the road of the same name before being culverted underneath the A491 at Moss Grove. On the western side of the A491 it passes the sites of the gas works and the Earl of Dudley's landsale coal wharf, and flows along the bottom of Barton Lane and Summerfield Avenue. It is culverted underneath the streets of the Valley Fields housing estate, the grounds of the former Ashwood House. The lake too has gone. The first houses were ready in the very early 1960s and the Briarwood properties in the seventies.

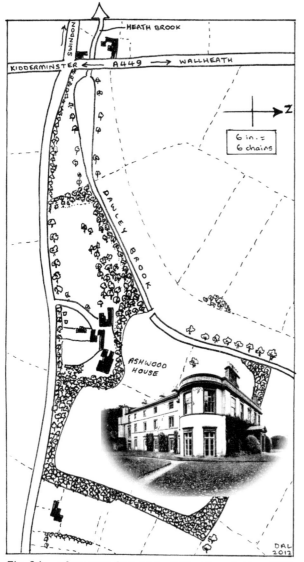

Fig. 84   FROM FOWLER'S MAP OF KINGSWINFORD, 1822

Ashwood House was built by the Earl of Dudley in the late eighteenth or very early nineteenth century. This was a popular spot for the well-to-do. White in his 1834 directory reports:

'a short distance from Summer Hill is Ashwood, an excellent house formerly occupied by Sir Joseph Scott' (10).

In 1834 Edward Dixon was the resident. Whilst the house and its grounds have been replaced by housing and whilst the brook has been culverted in a six feet diameter pipe, we still have the property details from the 1947 Himley Estates sale document:

*'**Ashwood House** - occupied for many years past as a Private Mental Home, having a valuable frontage of about 660 yards to Swindon Road and a return frontage of about 90 yards to Kidderminster Road.*

The House is built of brick with stuccoed elevations and slated roof and contains; -

On the Ground floor: - Vestibule porch; hall, with a very fine staircase, having the ends of each step finished in inlaid mahogany veneer, mahogany balustrade and inlaid handrail; Study, having Adam style doors and white marble mantelpiece; Lounge, having polished oak floor and white marble mantel, with flanking columns; Dining room, having oak floor, marble mantelpiece and door to pantry; Ladies' Dining room; Ladies' Sitting room No.1; Ladies' Sitting room No.2; Ladies' Small Dining room; Kitchen. Gents' Sitting Rooms, with lavatories adjoining; Pantries; Dairy and two sculleries.

120

On the First floor:- Bedroom No.1; Dressing room; Bedroom No2; Four dormitories; Bathroom; Ladies' bathroom; Matron's office; Two dormitories; Billiards room.

On the Second floor:- Three staff rooms; Sewing room; Linen room; Bathroom; and Five dormitories.

There are also excellent cellars.

The land is well timbered pasture and is intersected by the Dawley brook, which is dammed near the Kidderminster road to form a pool, having an area of 1.25 acres.

The whole, comprising 35 acres 0 roods and 26 poles is let to Dr WA O'Connor on a lease for 21 years from 25th March 1935, at an annual rent of £ 295-0s-0d.' (11)

A directory for 1900 informs us that:

'Ashwood House was the home of Dr James FG Pietersen and it is run as a private asylum.'

A very generous description of the house and grounds followed, with its location being pushed somewhat west:

'a large mansion, close upon the borders of Wales, with very well planted grounds, which are extremely picturesque" (12).

An Edwardian postcard shows the scene on the Kidderminster Road as the Dawley Brook becomes the Heathbrook. The farm on the opposite side of the road has been replaced by housing, but the water meadow remains. Within a few hundred yards the Heathbrook cuts underneath the Wall Heath to Swindon Road to re-emerge by the side of Severn-Trent's sewage pumping station. A meadow away are the pitches and clubhouse of Dudley Kingswinford Rugby Club, and backing that the remains of the embankment of the Shutt End Railway. The club, whose emblem is a lion, were given two stone lions for their entrance pillars, by Mr Nock, a former owner of Ellowes Hall, Sedgley. Each lion had a Biblical inscription upon it:

Left hand side
'Out of the eater came forth meat
Out of the strong came forth sweetness'

Right hand side
'The young lions roar after their prey
And seek their meat from God'

The first inscription is of course from Judges, Chapter 14, and verse 14. It portrays the story of Samson, his wife and the riddle he sets the Philistines. The second inscription is from Psalm 104, verse 21 and it is a meditation upon the mighty power and wonderful providence of God *(13)*.

The stone lions were stolen. Where are they now?

The rugby club's ground is aptly named Heathbrook, for the stream flows along its boundary. Originally the Heath Brook/Dawley Brook flowed into Flatheridge Pool before emptying into the Smestow. With the building of the Staffordshire and Worcestershire Canal and the need to have a basin at Ashwood for the transhipment of coal and other goods, a canal basin was built using the natural feature. The brook now flows into the marina, excess water being taken out of the canal at the weir at Rocky Lock.

Fig. 85   Ashwood Marina (Flatheridge Pool) from the canal

(1)   Remarks on the Puddling and Blast Furnaces. John Gibbons.
(2)   ibid 1.
(3)   ibid 1.
(4)   Whites directory and gazetteer of Staffordshire, 1834. P 265-6.
(5)   Britain in Old photographs Brierley Hill. Stan Hill, 1995. Alan Sutton Publishing. P93.
(6)   A History of the Pensnett Railway. WKV Gale, 1975. Goose and Son. P25.
(7)   The Friends of Kingswinford and Wall Heath Parks 2003-8 - The work of the Voluntary Group. JRS, Friends of the Parks, 2008. P6.
(8)   ibid 7.
(9)   ibid 7.
(10) ibid 4.
(11) The Himley Estates sale catalogue, January 14/15th 1947, Lot102. P55/6.
(12) Black Country Bugle, Annual 2006, quoting Kelly's Directory of Staffordshire, 1900.
(13) The Ellowes, its Owners and Times. Angus Dunphy, 1983. Dudley Teachers' Centre, item 7058.

Fig. 86

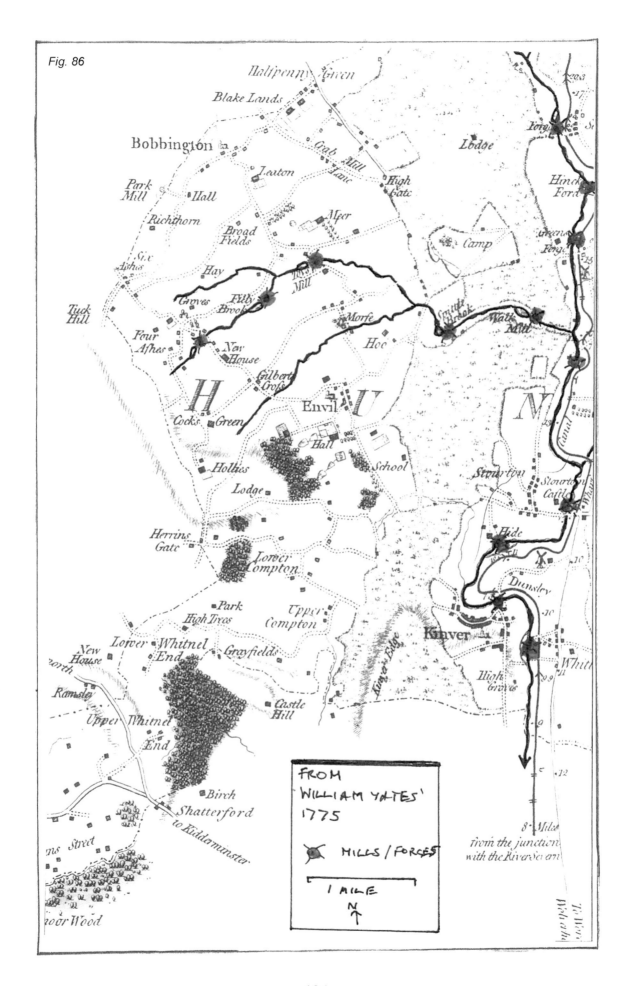

Halfpenny Green

Blake Lands

Bobbington

Oab Mill Lane

High Gate

Lodge

Forge

Hinck Ford

Park Mill

Hall

Leaton

Meer

Richthorn

Broad Fields

Camp

Forge

Six Ashes

Hay

Mill

Tuck Hill

Groves

Filly Brook

Morfe

Smith Brook

Walk Mill

N

Four Ashes

New House

Hoo

Gilbert Cross

H

U

Envil

Cocks Green

Hall

Stourton

Hollies

School

Stourton Castle

Lodge

Hide

Herring Gate

Lower Compton

Dunsley

Park

Upper Compton

High Trees

Kinver

New House

Lower

Whitnel End

Grayfields

Whitt

Ramsley

High Groves

Upper Whitnel End

Castle Hill

Birch

Shatterford

to Kiddarminster

Street

oor Wood

FROM WILLIAM YATES' 1775

MILLS / FORGES

1 MILE

N

8 Miles from the junction with the River Severn

124

These brooks cover one of the largest drainage basins in the Smestow system and flow through some of the loveliest countryside in South Staffordshire. The Philley and Sneyd's Brooks rise on the high ground of the Enville Sheepwalks, Coxgreen and Four Ashes. After their confluence they become the Spittle Brook. The Enville Brook joins the Spittle Brook a little lower down. At Checkhill a rivulet from the Highgate Common district comes in from the north, before the Spittle Brook exits through the Checkhill Gap, to join the Smestow River at Gothersley

The district is characterised by a series of wooded ridges which, west of the fault line from Mere Farm, Morfe Hall Farm and Enville Hall, eventually rise up to heights between 500 and 670 feet above sea level. The underlying rocks are composed of the Enville series of the Upper Coal Measures, which include sandstones, marls and hardy breccias. East of that fault the underlying geology forms part of the Trias group of

Fig. 87   Enville Sheepwalks

sandstones, which support both heath land with fern and birch coppices and wooded pebble bed escarpments. Scots pine are a native species characteristic of the district. By the time the Spittle Brook reaches Checkhill its gradient profile is slight. This has resulted in the alder marshes and oak woods of the Checkhill Bogs, which are a site of special scientific interest (SSSI).

The brooks once provided the power for corn milling, fulling (beating, stretching and producing cloth) and tool sharpening. Frequent mill ponds usually ensured an adequate supply of water. Few remain as most have been returned to meadow. A case could be made for keeping pools along the brooks' course, both for irrigation and for flood prevention purposes, as well as for sources of water supply for fire fighting in this heavily wooded area. The 2011 fires in the Million necessitated water being pumped from the Smestow.

For the size of the basin, stream flows are surprisingly limited, except in times of heavy rain and flood. The breaching of the Batch Pool dam on the Enville Estate, a few years ago, caused serious flooding at Checkhill, whilst in the very dry summer of 1976 the brook dried up. Local waterworks have significantly lowered the water table and taken a toll on many a cottage well. Supplies in the underground aquifer have been reduced and this has further encouraged a significant leakage through the stream bed in this sandstone country. The Victoria County History of Staffordshire Volume XX has the fullest story of mill sites along the brooks, whilst the later account by Cooksey and Cooksey has added to what we know.

The Philley Brook

This brook drains the area of land from west of the A458 Enville to Bridgnorth road, through the Four Ashes district in a north-easterly direction. The Philley Brook has two main arms. The northern one lies south of Hay Farm and for a distance marks the Enville/Bobbington parish boundary. The main brook rises west of Bradbury's Farm and the White Well and flows by way of The Toys and for a time parallel to Mere Lane.

It is surprising to note that the small Philley Brook supported three or four mills along its course. The first mill site was at The Toys. It belonged to Henry Wilcox of Lutley and at the time of his death in 1603 was known as Hay House Mill. His lands included those described as Walkmill Pool, which suggests that at some point there was a fulling mill. By 1638 John Toy of Lutley was working it as a corn mill. However there were two holdings connected with this mill. John gave his share of the property to his son, Edward (1), but it was to be another seventy or so years before both parts of the property were brought into single ownership. It was Henry Wollaston of Four Ashes Hall who achieved this in 1712. In fact there were two corn mills working in the same building and these he settled on his son. By mid century the mills were known as Lutley or the Lower Mills, although at the close of the eighteenth century only a single mill was working. Mr James Amphlett Grove of Four Ashes Hall bought the mill in 1829 (2). In 1834 John Fox of Lutley was the miller (3). The mill was still working in 1845 (4).

A little further downstream is the site of Philleybrook Mill (Fillibrook, Fillybrook). It lay south of Mere Lane and near to Philleybrook cottage. It was possibly the mill mentioned, along with other lands, in an indenture of 1447, which confirmed that ownership lay in the hands of the Bishop of Bath and Wells. It also noted that Robert Cole and his wife Katherine gave up all right to the property for a fee of 300 marks of silver (5). A similar type of agreement was signed in 1541, when Walter Wrottesley was confirmed as the rightful owner, together with numerous other lands and holdings. However, as part of the agreement Giles Strangeways, Knight, and his wife, Joan, gave up all their claims and accepted £340 in sterling (6). Philleybrook Mill was possibly the manor mill of Lutley. A lease dated 6th October 1624 for a messuage and a water corn mill, together with various lands was granted by Oliver and Thomas Whorwood (his son) of Lutley, to Norman Lee of Enville and Cox Green and Elizabeth, and their son Ambrose, for their natural lives for the sum of £144 (7). A hundred years later the mill had passed into the ownership of Joseph Amphlett of Four Ashes Hall and it was still held by this family in 1840 (8). Mr Geoffrey Smith of Wollaston, who is a direct descendant of the Toy family who have been associated with the parish for over three hundred years, remembers a building and a pool and his aunt talked of the building being lived in (9).

A third mill site lies where the public footpath (part of the Staffordshire Way) from Lutley and Mere Lane to Bendy's Wood and Morfe Lane crosses the brook. This was once the site of Lutley Mill. Mr Smith confirms that this site is known as Bumblehole. The mill site lies within the Enville Estate. Mr Frank Edwards of Spittlebrook Farm once ploughed the meadows hereabouts and he confirms that stonework was constantly being turned up and that it was a boggy site due to the clay. Nearby is the site of Lutley Manor house, with its outbuildings and fishponds.

Within a third of a mile is Mere Mill. It lies alongside the minor road that connects Mere and Morfe Lanes by way of Poolhouse Farm. Its story is complicated as it lay near to the boundary of the medieval manors of Lutley and Morfe, with both lordships keen to retain their rights. The story is further complicated as several people conjointly often held a part of Morfe Manor. Legal agreement was resorted to, so that documents could, in later years be used to prove title to the property. There are several pieces of evidence which remain and which help to tell the mill's story. The mill is located between Poolhouse and Morfe House Farms. This could be the site of the 1222 mill at Morfe: the latter farm is thought to be the site of the medieval Morfe Manor House, and in 1321 Philip de Lutley made an agreement with Henry Morfe, lord of part of the manor, over the exchange of lands which allowed Philip to extend his mill pond and alter the watercourses over Henry's land *(10)*. A year later Henry's widow claimed dower (a portion of a deceased husband's estate, which the law allowed her to keep for her lifetime). The dower included two mills and various lands and rents *(11)*.

In the years 1346, 1349, and 1362 Sir Fulk Birmingham, lord of the other part of Morfe manor, gave leases of the mill, which was called Aylewynes Mill or Hylewynesmilne to the Lord of Lutley *(12)*. A writ was made at Stourton in 1356, before John Swynnerton, the King's escheator (an official whose job it was to confiscate lands due to the King), by the oath of several local men: Richard de Enefeld, John ate Spyttle, William de la Hulle, Henry le Shepherde, Thomas Nyghtgale and others swore that John le Morfe, deceased, did not hold any lands or tenements in his demesne as of fee on his death and therefore there was nothing to escheat or confiscate. He did, however, hold one water mill and some small parcels of land and wood from 'Fulk de Burmyngham'. The mill was stated to be in a ruinous and dilapidated state *(13)*. On 24th June 1403 William Burnel, parson of Enville Church and others granted lands, tenements, rents and services, and a water mill in Morfe, held by the gift of Henry Morfe, to Henry Morfe and Katherine his wife and to Katherine his daughter *(14)*.

There are other references to Mere Mill. In 1442 both a corn and a fulling mill were operating under the same roof and were held of Lutley Manor. In 1496 Eleanor Strangeways Lady of Lutley, leased the mill which was then known as Aldwyns Mill to Stephen Toy, together with land called Walkmill Pool *(15)*.

The Toy family held the mill for most of the next three hundred years, until it was bought by WA Moseley, owner of the Mere Estate, in 1778 *(16)*. The mill was shown as Toys Mill on Yates' map of 1775 as well as in county directories *(17)* and it retained this name until the 1840s, by which time it took on the name Mere Mill. The Earl of Stamford bought the Mere Estate with Lutley manor from Walter Moseley in 1849 and with it the mill *(18)*. William Hainsworth was the miller and he is still recorded as such in 1851 *(19)*. By the 1870s William Mansell is listed as both farmer and miller at Mere Mill *(20)*, but in 1891 William Webster is shown as the occupant *(21)*. From the early 1890s and well into the twentieth century it is the name of Dorrell that is associated with the tenancy *(22)*.

The current, three-storey mill building probably dates to the late eighteenth century and the evidence of occasional pieces of sandstone in its lower walls would support this. Grain was taken into the top floor, and stored or emptied directly into one of two hoppers. From these it was tipped down chutes, which each fed one of the two pairs of stones on the milling floor below. On this floor there is a header tank, which was fed via a culvert that passed underneath the road from the mill pool. The water from the tank was piped onto the top of, or 'overshot', the mill wheel, which lay alongside the eastern side of the building. This great iron wheel had:

'...a diameter of 11 feet x 3 feet eight inches wide. It had eight iron arms, but the shaft, sole boards, shrouds and buckets were wooden' (23).

The mill ceased working in the 1930s and the water wheel has gone, but the wheel-arch in the building and a great deal of the machinery inside still remains.

The millwrights engineered their plant to provide the most effective use of the available power and of the machinery, through a gearing system like that discussed in chapter 11. The ground floor contains an eight-arch cast iron pit wheel with a diameter of six feet, formerly connected by its axle to the external mill wheel. It has 80 cogs, which meshed with 40 on the 3ft diameter cast iron wallower, the gear that surrounds the vertical main shaft. The wallower therefore had to make two revolutions to every one of the pit wheel, rotating the upright shaft (which is eight-sided, on this floor) at this faster pace, i.e. a ratio of 2:1. Above the wallower is the great spur wheel, again made of cast iron and with a diameter of six feet three inches. Its speed was determined by that of the shaft, while its 120 cogs meshed with the 28-30 cogs of the two small gears (one of these is missing) known as stone nuts. These were of cast iron with wooden pegs, and revolved at four times the speed of the shaft. They drove the iron rods which are still connected to the millstones on the floor above. The rods turned the two sets of stones, which are of four feet diameter. One of the stones has fallen through to the ground floor, but three remain in situ.

The main shaft passes on up through the milling floor. As the machinery has been left untouched for decades, it is of no surprise to learn that the heavy wooden shaft has dropped by about a foot and is therefore now out of true. It is sixteen-sided on the milling floor, and around it here is a 5ft diameter wooden crown wheel, with approximately 60 pegs. These cogged onto and

Fig. 88   Lay shaft, crown wheel & main shaft head, with header tank (rear left)

drove a cast iron, 1ft 2in diameter, fifteen-cog bevel gear; this therefore moved at four times the speed of the crown wheel, and drove the horizontal lay shaft which operated the sack hoist, allowing bags of grain or flour to be moved up and down through the mill. Other machines such as oat crushers would have been driven from the belt drums along the lay shaft.

Fig 89   Inside Mere Mill

The four images at left are arranged relatively, to show the layout of the milling operation in the building. From top to bottom:

– *The top floor: the two grain hoppers are seen either side of the exterior door.*

– *The milling floor: chutes lead from the hoppers above to the two sets of millstones, one pair of which (right) remains intact.*
Here the crown wheel around the main shaft drove the horizontal lay shaft with its belt drums, via the small bevel gear.

– *The ground floor: the horizontal great spur wheel drove the stone nuts (one remains at back right), which connected to the millstones above. Beneath it is the much smaller wallower, which meshed with the large vertical pit wheel, also shown in the bottom picture in the sequence.*

– *The pit wheel sits on its massive axle still, which would have also carried the external water wheel originally.*

Throughout the lower three photos, the amount that the main shaft has dropped out of alignment over the decades of inactivity can be seen.

Below is the view down through the semi-collapsed milling floor, showing the vertical drop to the great spur wheel and then the wallower further beneath.

Fig. 90   Inside Mere Mill

Left: the author counts the 'teeth' on the mill's crown wheel

Centre: three of the millstones; one intact pair (left) and one fallen through to the ground floor (right). Note larger blocks here in exterior wall, behind rubble at the left of shot, which are sandstone

Bottom: the well-preserved lay shaft, with its bevel gear (far end), drum for the sack hoist chain and belt drums (near camera)

130

The mill is private property and not open to the public. The mill pond has been drained and planted with commercial poplar trees.

Fig. 91   Mere Mill

Sneyd's Brook

The word Sneyd occurs in several places in Staffordshire and usually refers to a district which is a part or fragment of a larger whole; a district which is outlying, detached, or a privileged part of a manor. This meaning might fit as the brook separates Morfe manor from Enville Manor on the south and Lutley Manor on the north *(24)*.

Sneyd's Brook rises in several places between Coxgreen, Essex Wood and the Enville Sheepwalks. It feeds a number of pools to the west of Leigh House Farm on the Enville Estate, before crossing the A458 Stourton to Bridgnorth road. It then flows parallel to Morfe Lane, through Church Gorse, in a north-easterly direction to Morfe Hall Farm, Hoo Farm and its confluence with the Philley Brook at grid reference 834881.

Sneyd's and a stream (not part of the Smestow system) called the Mill Brook are very much part of the Enville Hall property, already famous by the 1740s for its gardens, walks and water features. Marshall in his two-volume study of Planting and Rural Ornament has this to say of the grounds:

'The immediate site is the precipitous face of an extended hill broken into furrows and watered by rills. The site contains several hundred acres which are divided chiefly into sheep walk and coppice wood, with kept grounds near the house, with meadows and arable lands round the church and village' (25).

He goes on to comment on the *'splendour of the water and its features, including a cascade and many lakes and ponds'.*

In the mid-nineteenth century the grounds of Enville Hall were even more splendid, and the fetes of the 1850s are famous in Black Country folklore as the Earl of Stamford and Warrington threw open his grounds to a very mixed public.

The main lakes above the house are fed by the headwaters of the Mill Brook. There was a mill at Lyndon, on the Spring pools, from Tudor times until at least the 1750s. On leaving the Home Farm the brook swings east and then south to join the River Stour south of Potters Cross, Kinver. At the end of the last ice age the course of this brook, and another called the Little Brook that drains from Compton and joins it beyond Heathlands, were diverted by fluvioglacial-laid deposits of gravel. Instead of flowing north to Enville Common, the Checkhill Gap and the River Smestow, their waters were captured by the Stour.

In more recent time Ida Mary Downing of Stourton Hall published two books of poetry, with the title *Close Downs*. The poems were read in the 1920s by the BBC broadcaster, Percy Edgar, as epilogues at the closedown each evening of station 5 IT. One is entitled 'The Sheep Walks' and is reproduced here.

'Behind the greyness of the hills, that stretch
In undulating lines, like some great wave,
Poised there, then petrified in it's descent,
The sun smiles down in love, on a fair world,
Of thinning forest trees, of meadowlands,
Upon a stately home, where clinging leaves,
Redden in greeting to the dying year,
Here, sunsets glow and fade as in a dream,
That mingles with the rapture of the Dawn!' (26).

The waters of Sneyd's Brook fed the wheels of two mills. The first was at Morfe Hall Farm, thought to have existed by the beginning of the sixteenth century. There was certainly a mill at this site by 1609. In 1698 Edward Hawkes held it and it was known by the family name for at least the next sixty years. William Yates does not show either Morfe or Hoo mills on his 1775 county map. This is not surprising for he fails to note mills elsewhere. He did, however, give an impression of the large number of mills in both the Enville district and the county as a whole. By the early 1980s there was still evidence of the mill pool, but this is now no more than a soggy valley bottom.

The second mill was situated at Hoo Farm a little distance downstream. James Parrish is shown as the miller in directories of the 1840-50s *(27)*. The mill pool is shown on the 1887 6-inch OS sheet, but not the mill. This is still the case in 1904. Apparently there were traces of a building at the northern corner of the pool near to the house in 1982 (28). A pond for irrigation now occupies the approximate site. The name Hoo simply means hill and usually is associated with a single isolated homestead, which is raised up above the valley floor.

The Enville Brook

A rivulet, which for want of a better name we shall refer to as the Enville Brook, flows from the Enville Hall Estate, nearby to the site of Stamford House, and heads south of Blundies and Commonside to join the Spittle Brook upstream of Spittlebrook Mill.

The Spittle Brook (together with the Highgate Brook)

Spittlebrook is thought to derive its name from the Knights Hospitallers, who were granted six acres of land in Kinver Forest, free of forest laws, by Richard I in 1189 *(29)*. The Spittle Brook, its waters increased by the confluence of the Philley and Sneyd Brooks, flows west towards the Checkhill Gap. Hereabouts the brook is near to, or forms, the parish boundary between Enville and Kinver. Before the land completely closes in there are features worthy of note.

Spittlebrook Mill was one of the principal mills of the district. The mill itself lies just inside Enville parish, but the adjacent Georgian mill house, now the farmhouse, is in Kinver parish. Both are substantial buildings. Today, Mr Frank Edwards and his family run Mill Farm at Spittlebrook.

Mills were often known by the name of the miller and this could continue long after he had left the mill. This was the case with Spittlebrook Mill. Mrs Theresa Edwards reports that when a beam was removed from over the kitchen range old invoices bearing the name Fox were found – the mill was still known as Foxes Mill right up to the First World War, although the Allsopps were the millers here from 1872 (if not before) until 1919 *(30)*. They in their turn left their name, for the older generation refer to it still. It is thought the Fox family emigrated to Canada.

At various times it was a fulling, corn and blade mill, changing and re-changing its use as economic opportunities altered. *The Victoria County History* charts the history of the mill. It seems likely that it was the fulling mill operated by Roger Higgs in 1516. The mill was still known as Higgs Mill in 1728. It was granted by John Grey, Lord of Enville, to Richard Lee of the Hoo in 1574. Richard Lee granted his mill to Thomas Leigh of Leigh House in 1580 and by 1603 it had become a blade mill. By mid-century it seems it was operating as a corn mill, but by the early eighteenth century it was working as a fulling mill again *(31)*. William Baker of Tong Norton granted its lease to Bramwell Powell of Greensforge in 1747/8 for £13 per annum for a term of 29 years *(32)*. In 1817 its use had reverted to corn milling. Charles Foster Cotterill, William Cotterill and Luke Tipton were the lessees in 1844 *(33)*. Lord Stamford bought it in April 1849 from Gilbert Brown and sometime after it was rebuilt *(34)*. At this stage it was known as Spittlebrook Mill. It continued to work into the twentieth century, its activity gradually declining and finally ceasing in 1919.

A delightful account of the Spittlebrook country is captured for us in OA Merritt Hawkes' book *The Cottage by the Common*, published in 1924 and reflecting this district at the time of the First World War. Her words reflect not only the countryman's dislike of millers, whether justified or not, but also a prophetic understanding of the economy of milling early in the twentieth century. She writes:

'Across the fields is another pool made by a miller from the little stream. There, for hundreds of years the water turned the stones to grind the corn of the neighbourhood. In payment the miller took a certain amount from each sack. When he had grown rich enough to build himself a great brick house folk said he had become rich by taking more than his due share - but he clung too long to the water mill and his old stones, so his business passed to the men in the city, whose steam mills made a finer and whiter flour.

The water wheel is very green now. It goes but rarely and then only to grind corn for cattle. Its day is nearly over. The last miller is thin and white and bent, and near his end, but the little stream goes on, and the grass grows as if time were not.

The mill pond too has had its day. Once it was kept clean, but now it is full of water weeds and flowers. At one end the reeds have it all their own way, but along one side the flags have made a fragrant home, and just beyond, the peppermint grows rank strong. There are moorhens in abundance. In the dusk they run across the weed-strewn water, or in the meadow among the kingcups and the meadowsweet.

One day a miller was found in the pond. The village said it was a suitable end for a bad old man. The water mill is old, but when it looks up at the hill and sees the ruin of the old windmill, perhaps it feels quite young and modern.

We can still climb up to the windmill by an overgrown track in which broom and heather grow, sheltering the nests of birds and mice. Seventy years ago, and years before then, this track was wide enough for the carts that took corn up one day and on another brought down the resulting flour, brown and wholesome and a real staff of life.

The old windmill is a landmark for miles. The windows and floors have gone and its shiplike moving top gets less with each winter gale; but the thick walls still remain, their worst enemies being the swallows, who carry away the mortar. Its day is long since past, but it is not quite alone, for at its feet is its descendant, the watermill. The two generations live together in the country, but the next generation is a huge steam mill far away in the city. Industries as well as people have deserted the country' (35).

The water mill, built of red brick with blue brick window lintel and sill decoration and with a central cupola, consists of five bays and four floors (ground, first, second, third); at first the visitor sees three storeys to the mill, but quickly realises that there is a ground floor below dam level. Carts were unloaded and loaded at the north gable end. Above them, a chain hoist lifted the sacks of grain up to the door on the third floor to be taken into the mill, whilst the same chain was used to lower the sacks of ground oats and flour from the first floor to the waiting carts below – the chain was operated by tightening or loosening the pulley, depending on whether an upwards or downwards movement was required. The second floor was divided into four very large storage areas, or garners. As required the corn was tipped into chutes, dropping it to the first floor, where two pairs of millstones approximately four feet in diameter were at work. These are now found elsewhere in the district.

Mr. Frank Edwards

Fig. 92   Spittlebrook Mill and farm, past and present

The mill was unusual, for it had an internal water wheel, an overshot iron structure of approximately ten feet diameter and four feet width, with wooden buckets that were fed by a sluice in the dam wall. The millrace once ran in the narrow defile between house and mill. From the mill wheel a pit wheel cogged onto the wallower, which was itself attached to the main axle tree. Cogs and rods provided the power to drive the millstones, pulleys and other machinery (36).

The breaking of the massive main shaft – in effect a huge tree trunk – which passed up through the building signalled the end of milling. After corn milling had ceased, sawmilling continued for a time. The mill machinery was removed for scrap in 1967. Today, the bottom floor of the mill building is used as a shelter for cattle, the first floor as a workshop, the second floor as a grain store still, whilst the top floor is redundant. All the floors above the ground floor still have their sharply rising staircases in situ.

The lines of the mill pond and some brickwork can be clearly seen in the dam wall. The mill pond was still in evidence until the late 1950s, but the silting up of the leat on the downstream side of where it returned water to the main stream effectively heralded its end. Mr Frank Edwards (now a sprightly 91) returned the pond to meadow. He and his family continue to farm some two hundred or so acres from Spittlebrook, at Mill Farm (37). They can reflect that grandfather, Hubert, and his father came here in 1919 as tenants of the Enville Estate and that they carry on that proud tradition of producing food for the nation.

Beyond this farm, a tributary joins from the north. It will be helpful if we call it the Highgate Brook, for it flows from this direction. It has cut across Enville Golf Club's lands (My Lady's Farm). It once filled a large pool and the long slender Foucher's (Poucher's) Pool, both drained, before cutting south through Lodge Plantation, the Bogs Covert and Little Checkhill Plantation.

During World War One the western side of the woodland of My Lady's Farm was cleared of scrub, ploughed and planted with barley. The old charcoal burner was at work here, as well as in the Hampton Valley on the other side of the gap, felling oak, elm, chestnut, beech and pine, and all for the war effort (38).

Ida Mary Downing has also commemorated the passing of the woods of Hampton Valley in her poem of the same name:

'Below the hill, on which our cottage stood,
Grew, in unrivalled beauty, sombre, grand,
The great primeval monarchs of the wood
Piercing, with mighty roots, the dry, red, sand.
One day I heard the woodman's even blows,
And wondering, stood to see the murder done,
..." (39).

The tiny stream was probably fed by underground seepages from Highgate Common, where according to Merritt Hawkes: 'there is a round pool of clear, cool water. The sandy bottom can be seen. The swallows love the pool. That pond is our bathing pool' (40). Highgate Common is a designated Country Park –

Fig. 93   CHECKHILL AREA c. 1904

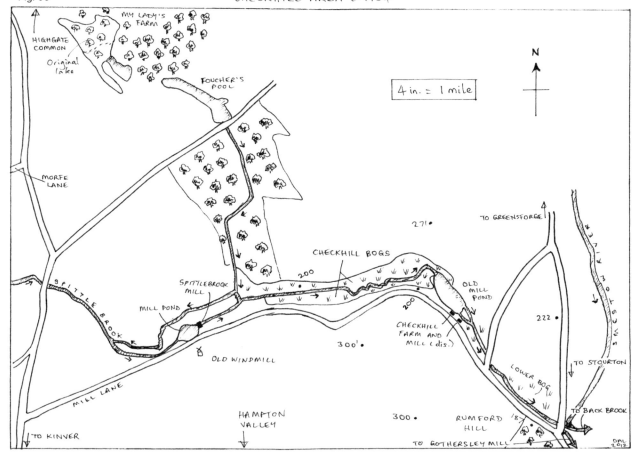

Staffordshire County Council bought it off the Enville Estates. It was first registered as common land under the Commons Registration Act in the late 1960s. The pool is still in evidence, unlike the large lake and Foucher's Pool on My Lady's Farm, which are also described by Hawkes:

'There is one large lake enough for boats. It is almost surrounded by trees- on one side there are oaks and alders, and on the other, firs and birches. The glory of this lake is the wild cherry tree, which leans over the water as if the better to see its whiteness in the spring and its scarlet in the autumn. Here wild ducks find a safe home, swimming with moorhens and a few coots. Some years kingfishers flash here and there, shaking the air with their load musical cry.

This lake had a sister, smaller and more beautiful, for it was long and narrow. To the west there were a few pine trees, between whose trunks the setting sun sent its golden orange rays. This lake was at its best in July, when its blue waters were ringed about by tall yellow ragwort, the yellow appearing even brighter against the background of dark pines. The lake was a turquoise set in gold. The lake has been drained'.

After the confluence of the Highgate Brook the Spittle Brook enters the area known as the Checkhill Bogs. This is an area of special scientific interest. It consists of two distinct wet woodland areas consisting of alder and oak woodland separated by an old, but extensive, mill pond. Unfortunately the bog is drying out and South Staffordshire Water, in its management plan, proposes by 2015 to reduce water extraction at Ashwood Pumping Station to alleviate the problem. The wood lark, with its short tail and its sweet song, was once a resident here, as it

Fig. 94   Checkhill Bogs

was over much of Enville's sandy heath. A rare ground-nesting bird, it raises two clutches of about four eggs. Its nest, richly lined with moss and horse hair, is built in a depression, sheltered by bramble, bracken or tree.

An ice lobe, moving eastwards, probably created the Checkhill Gap, by cutting through the Bunter Pebble bed ridge *(41)*. The Spittle Brook follows this course. A heronry is found in the upper bog, before the large millpond is reached. This once fed the important mill of Checkhill. Like Spittlebrook Mill, this place has seen a variety of activity – the present eighteenth-century mill building is but the latest in what must have been a succession of mill buildings, mill use and mill sites.

In the late sixteenth century there was a blade mill here, which had been worked by Francis Penn and/or Edward Meeke. In 1601 it was given up by Richard Bate to Humphrey Jordan *(42)*. The Victoria County History fills in the ownership for us. It appears that Jordan held two blade mills at Checkhill in 1625 and that in 1628 Richard Burneford, who was living at Checkhill, is named as a scythegrinder. Other scythegrinders are named, one being Francis Bennett, who died in 1666. The Bennetts were here until 1683, when apparently Philip Foley granted a twenty-one-year lease to Thomas Wannerton, a scythegrinder *(43)*. He was still there in 1689, but ten years later the mill's use had been turned to fulling. John Heath was working it at this time. It was subsequently held by John Install in the 1730s and by Thomas Arnott in 1789. Yates' map of 1775 confirms Checkhill's use for fulling, naming it as Walk Mill. Large areas were required for tenters, or hooks, so that the cloth could be walked, stretched and dried. As the Kinver cloth industry changed so too did the use of the mill, which started corn milling at about this time *(44)*.

The Burgess family are associated with Checkhill Mill throughout the nineteenth century. George, who died in 1824, was succeeded by his son, George. He was a tenant of JH Hodgetts-Foley of Prestwood and is still shown as farmer and miller in the directories up to the 1860s *(45)*. The mill appears to have worked up until the 1880s. This is borne out by directory entries which only mention farmer, rather than farmer and miller. For much of the 1890s J Horton was the farmer at Checkhill. He was followed by Elizabeth Lees in 1899 and very quickly afterwards by John Burgess Adams, who was still there during the First World War *(46)*.

Charles Percy Wilkes, known as Walter, took the farm in 1926 and the family have worked the 450 acres ever since, giving both a commitment to the land and the district. The fourth generation, through David, are now making a further contribution. After milling had ceased the mill was used to work farm machinery by a series of rods. Charles Wilkes, the present farmer, and Walter's son, recollects his father telling him that when he came to Checkhill, the mill supplied electricity for the farm.

Fig. 95   Checkhill Mill, including surviving machinery and millstones

As one of the buckets was missing on the mill wheel the lights would momentarily flutter. Electricity was supplied into the 1930s *(47)*.

Cooksey and Cooksey in their 1986 survey included a 1972 photograph of the mill wheel. It was of the overshot type, 9 feet 8 inches in diameter and 4 feet wide, fed by a header tank *(48)*. The wheel lay alongside a relatively small building of 20 feet by 12 feet, but what the building lacked in size it made up for with three floors (the large mill pond suggests that previous mill structures were larger). However, this mill may first have been used for fulling, before it was converted to a corn mill. The wheel was made of iron with wooden buckets. Some equipment, including several pulleys, remains in situ inside the mill suggesting how the mill was worked. The mill wheel would have connected with a flat pit wheel, which drove a pinion on a lay shaft with an iron pulley. This would have operated a line shaft with pulleys *(49)*, whose belts would have driven two pairs of stones, as well as farm machinery, by a series of rods stretching across the yard. Today a set of stones grace the farmhouse garden. The mill wheel lies beneath the made up ground at the side of the mill.

Of the three floors, the basement housed the pit wheel, whilst milling took place on the ground floor. Grain was hoisted to the upper floor and was rolled, before being fed onto the millstones (the rolling equipment again suggests the former use of fulling). Today only the top floor is used, as the ground floor is unsafe and has partly fallen into the basement.

The substantial dam allows the brook to drain through a deep sandstone channel on the north side, which cuts through the pebble beds.

After Checkhill Farm the Spittle Brook flows through the lower bogs to meet the Smestow at the Rumford crossroads. A rivulet has joined flowing off Rumford Hill. At one time a leat passed underneath the Smestow, flowing to Gothersley to feed the ponds of the ironworks.

Fig. 96   Confluence of Spittle Brook with Smestow Brook

(1)   Victoria County history of Staffordshire Vol XX, 1984. P111-2.
(2)   The VCH gives a footnote referring to a manuscript at Four Ashes Hall-bundle 4-, which is an abstract of title to Lutley Farm and Mill. VCH P104 - Four Ashes Estate passed through the Wollastons to the Amphletts by the marriage of Elizabeth Wollaston to Joseph Amphlett in 1725. Their son Joseph died unmarried but his nephew James Amphlett Grove acquired the estate. He died unmarried in 1854.
(3)   White's History, Gazetteer and Directory of Staffordshire, 1834. P258.
(4)   PO Directory of Staffordshire. 1845.
(5)   Staffordshire Historical Collections (SHC) Vol XI, 1890. P229.
(6)   ibid 5 P282.
(7)   Enville Estate Archives. B1/1/20.
(8)   ibid 1.
(9)   Mr Geoffrey Smith, direct descendant of the Toy family.
(10) ibid 1 and Enville Estate Archives A/6/5
(11) ibid 5 P38.
(12) ibid 1 and Enville Estate Archives A/6/10.
(13) SHC, 1913. P162-3.
(14) Enville Estate Archives A/6/18
(15) ibid 1.
(16) ibid 1.
(17) William Yates' map 1775; White's Directory 1834, P258; 1851, P176; VCH, P111.
(18) ibid 1 P105
(19) White's Directories 1834, P258, and 1851, P176.
(20) PO Directory of Staffordshire 1872 P602 and 1022.
(21) Stourbridge Almanac and Directory 1891.
(22) ibid 19 for years 1893-1917 and Kelly's Directory of Staffordshire 1912, P176 and 1924, P188.
(23) Watermills and Water-powered Works on the River Stour, Worcestershire and Staffordshire part 5: Smestow Brook. SM Cooksey and MV Cooksey. 1986. P15.
(24) Notes on Staffordshire Place Names. WH Duignan 1902. P140. Henry Frowde, London.
(25) Planting and Rural Ornament. Marshall, 1746. P327-334. G Nichol Bookseller.
(26) Close Down and Other Poems. Ida Mary Downing, 1926. P106. Munns and Allen.
(27) PO Directory 1845; White's 1851, P176.
(28) ibid 1.
(29) VCH. P137.
(30) ibid 19 and PO Directory 1872, P602 and 1021; Kelly's Directory 1912. P176 and 856.
(31) ibid 1.
(32) Enville Estate Archives B/1/12
(33) ibid 32
(34) ibid 1 and ibid 32
(35) The Cottage by the Common. OA Merritt Hawkes, 1924. P144-6. Williams and Norgate Ltd.
(36) Information Mr Frank and Mrs Theresa Edwards, farmers at Spittlebrook Mill Farm.
(37) ibid 30
(38) ibid 30. P189-190; Information Mr Thomas Preece of Enville, 1973.
(39) ibid 24 P155.
(40) ibid 30 P141.
(41) Geology of the Country between Dudley and Bridgnorth, 1947. P172. HMSO.
(42) ibid 1 P147.
(43) ibid 1 P147.
(44) ibid 1 P148.
(45) White's Directory 1851. P180.
(46) ibid 20.
(47) Evidence Mr Charles Wilkes.
(48) ibid 9 P14, 18.
(49) ibid 9 P14.

Fig. 97

HINKSFORD MILL TO RUMFORD COVERT

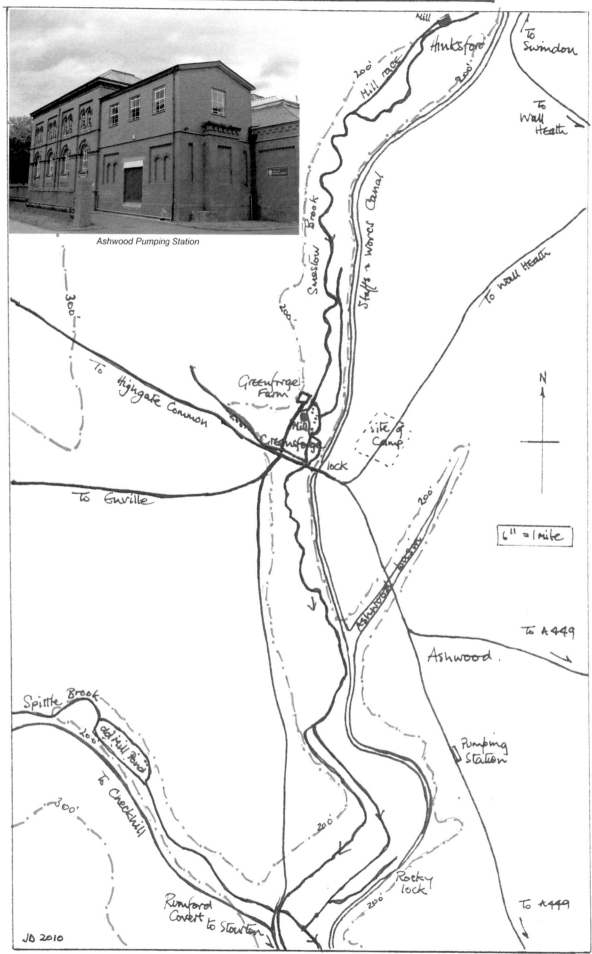

Ashwood Pumping Station

JD 2010

The valley at Hinksford is the site of a large and pleasant mobile home and caravan park. It was set up by Seisdon Rural District Council in the 1950s. The river will only fall some thirty-three feet over the next four miles, and although it carries a greater volume of water the rate of flow is considerably reduced in some reaches, as it meanders its way to join the Stour. This has allowed alder marshes to flourish in the poorly drained valley bottoms.

Fig. 98   The Smestow near Greensforge

The west bank is dominated by Greensforge Rough, where trees cling to the near-precipitous edge. On the valley's eastern flank is the line of the Roman road, on its way from Pennocrucium to Greensforge military fort. It cuts across the Mile Flat. This was the frontier of Rome's law in the period AD 47-61, as two forts and three marching camps testify. These were troubled times in Britain, with Rome trying to establish itself against a backcloth of change of emperor, of provincial governor and of policy. The British uprising in the east of the country was the result, but all areas were unstable for a time. The two forts (the second and larger fort replaced the former) were well sited in the neck of land above the marshy Smestow and Dawley Brook valleys.

From this military hub a network of roads radiated outwards; to the south to the salt settlement of Droitwich; to the north to Pennocrucium and Watling Street; to the north west through Bank Farm, Whitehouse and Blackhills Woods to Rudge Heath and Uxacona (Oakengates); and westwards via Bobbington and Broughton to the Severn valley and eventually to Craven Arms. There must also have been a road to the east along the Mile Flat and through Wall Heath, before it climbed onto the South Staffs plateau. Evidence, however, remains to be found. Wall Heath has taken its first name from the word meaning an earth rampart, whilst 'heath' refers to the later heathland settlement in medieval Kinver Forest. Not enough importance is given to Greensforge's role in the period before the Roman frontier moved west and before a more settled existence was established under Roman occupation.

Fig. 99   Greensforge road bridge

Within living memory the Mile Flat (not actually a straight mile) was an unofficial testing ground for Wolverhampton-built motor cycles and cars. Greensforge is a pleasant watering hole, the Navigation Inn being a

Fig. 100   Greensforge Mill

popular venue for a pub lunch. Nearby is the four-storey corn mill. The mill closed in the 1920s, but Enville Estates have created a series of apartments within the disused mill building and turned adjacent outbuildings into attractive offices. This has preserved the architecture of this late-Victorian complex for future generations. A five-foot head of water fed the wheel, the size of the wheel pit suggesting that the wheel was fourteen feet by approximately twelve feet six inches wide. The mill machinery drove four pairs of stones *(1)*.

The harnessing of the Smestow River at this site took place over many centuries. King *(2)* suggests that a finery forge was probably built here in 1599. Mr Green, who operated the forge in this period, has left us his name. Greensforge was one of four forges worked by Dud Dudley from the early 1620s. Between 1668 and 1673 it was operated by Richard Gray for Philip Foley, along with Swin and Heath. In these years it produced between 101 and 135 tons of bar iron per annum, slightly more than its two neighbours *(3)*. Mr Charles Wilkes reports that iron slag, with heavy iron content, is turned up by the plough in his field to the south of the road, and west of the brook, at Greensforge, thus showing that the processes then available resulted in a heavy wastage of materials *(4)*. The three forges were described as:

'very beneficial works, being well watered and convenient to Grange furnace for pigs and to the market for sale. The ways are good which saves abundance in carriage. They are in good repair and have no or but little watercourse rents to charge the owner. They lie near pitcoal for drawing out iron. Hearthstones are available from Himley and limestone from the Wrens Nest'. *(5)*.

However, Philip knew how to talk up his works for in 1675 he leased Greensforge to Sir Clement Clerke and John Finch and in the next half a dozen years to a succession of speculative forge masters. It had closed by 1686. Subsequently the plant was converted to a blade mill/s, let to Francis Patchett in 1707, in whose family it remained until at least 1789. Benjamin Beddard occupied the site at its sale in 1826 *(6)*. One source claims that there were two mills, with one being converted to a corn mill by 1733; the blade mill was still working in 1841 *(7)*. In the nineteenth century the Beddards were millers at Hinksford's Hollow Mill and there may well be a connection with Benjamin. The structure we see today replaced the previous corn mill in the 1890s.

144

Nearby Chasepool, or Greens, Lodge was the home of Mr Green. It was from here that he controlled his forge. Later Dud Dudley held a lease on it from his father.

As the river leaves Greensforge there is a coppice beyond its western bank. On the edge of the wood is a cave. John Mason, a 'gentleman of the road', regularly used the sandstone cave in the 1940s and 1950s and this was his preferred home. He tramped the district, sometimes staying at the Rock Cottages at Heathmill, or in the cave in Swindon Rough. These were the days a village looked after its own, so when the Wombourne doctor was passing the Rock Cottages he would leave a bottle of medicine in the grass. Kind to the children, who were always pleased to see him, John lies buried in Himley churchyard, taking his secrets with him. He died of hypothermia in 1958 and was found in a linesman's hut on the Wombourne Railway at Himley. Recently, through the generosity of local people a gravestone has been erected to this gentle and, many suspect, well-educated man (8).

The Staffordshire and Worcestershire Canal Navigation partners the Smestow through much of its journey and along this final stretch of the river it is a very close companion. And, so to Ashwood! In medieval times Ashwood Hay was a small enclosure in the Royal Forest of Kinver. It was managed by a head forester living at Prestwood. From here he enforced the forest laws for the protection of both the woodland cover and the King's deer. Chasepool was another of the hays of Kinver Forest.

In the seventeenth century Philip Foley enclosed some lands, bringing them into the Prestwood estate, and Lord Dudley granted leases effectively bringing much of Ashwood Hay into his control. The late eighteenth century saw enclosure on a massive scale, through the Ashwood Hay (1776) and Kingswinford (1784) Enclosure Acts. The chief beneficiary was Lord Dudley, who was confirmed as the major landowner in the district. Thus, his agents were in a position to exploit the mineral wealth of Pensnett Chase and adjacent areas. Flatheridge Pool lay at the confluence of the Dawley and Smestow Brooks. It was developed into an extensive canal basin, which we know as Ashwood. An eleven-arch brick and sandstone viaduct today straddles the valley of the Dawley Brook and carries the road from Greensforge to Lawnswood over Ashwood Marina.

With the development of the Himley/Shutt End coalfield, an agreement was reached between Mr James Foster and Lord Dudley, which enabled the raw materials present to be exploited. The agreement signed on 27th January, 1827 reads:

'Lord Dudley to make and maintain a railway from a meadow adjoining the Staffordshire and Worcestershire Canal called Flatheridge Meadow being No. 6 on Mr Fowlers map of the parish of Kingswinford to certain land, belonging to him in the occupation of Joseph Cox near to the church at Kingswinford and adjoining certain lands belonging to John Hodgetts Hodgetts Foley Esquire now under lease to Mr James Foster for the conveyance of coal limestone ironstone and other materials and articles The railway to be made according to a plan and section thereof as lately made by Mr John Urspeth Rastrick Civil Engineer and to be found and constructed in a suitable manner and adapted to the use of steam engines to be employed in propelling the carriages to be used thereon" (9).

Fig. 101

RUMFORD COVERT TO STOURBRIDGE CANAL

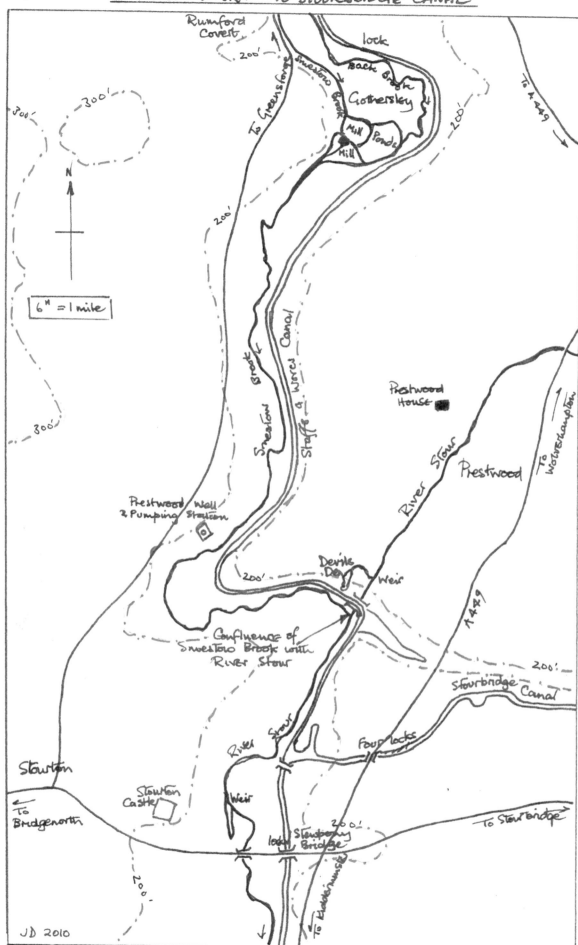

JD 2010

Beyond the Marina is Ashwood, the first waterworks built by the South Staffordshire Company in the Smestow Valley. In 1893 the Earl of Dudley, fearful that his workers on the coalfield lost too many days of work through sickness, approached the company and offered to sell them the Ashwood site for £2000 per acre. Marten and Witham-King of the Dudley and Midland Geological Society submitted a report. The Ashwood works was to confirm their views that abundant supplies lay untapped. Eventually six boreholes reached the Bunter Pebble Beds and yielded four million gallons daily. The water is pumped to Dudley (10). Unusually the station was equipped with horizontal compound engines of the non-rotating type, supplied by Hathorn Davey of Leeds. They operated until 1959 (11), after which electric pumps replaced them. Up until then coal was transported from Ashwood Basin by cart.

However, a note of caution is in order for whilst it has been claimed that the valley could supply 20 million gallons of water daily, the Wolverhampton plants extract about 5 million gallons and the South Staffs plants about 9.5 million. Other nearby plants such as Kinver need factoring in. The water table has been lowered thereby affecting river flow, as a considerable amount of water is lost through its bed. Wetland areas such as Checkhill have suffered.

Nearby is the very busy and popular garden centre, attracting visitors from a wide area and providing employment for local people.

A little further south is Gothersley, the site of a seventeenth-century blade mill/s, possibly from as early as 1670. It may have been built by Philip Foley and was occupied until 1691 by James Raybould, a prominent scythe smith. Foley then leased the mill to William Webb, a scythe grinder, for a term of ninety-nine years. It was William who built the access road from Ashwood Lane, a bridge over the Smestow and a house for himself at Gothersley. His widow Jane was running the blade mill in 1716, but by the 1730s it had been rebuilt as a slitting mill (12). Here, bar iron was split into rods. The mill was first worked by Francis Homfray and after his death, in 1737, by Mary his widow. It remained in the family for most of the eighteenth century: John Hodgetts, who had married Elizabeth Foley of Prestwood, leased it to Francis's son, Francis, and his two sons, Francis and Jeston (13).

Ten years later widow Elizabeth Foley leased Gothersley Slitting mill for £100 per annum to her husband's nephew, who was also called John. This John formed a partnership with John Thompson and John Scale and this and their other works soon began to prosper. John, newly married, and with a month old daughter, died tragically whilst swimming in a pool near to his Aberdare works in South Wales. His widow, Elizabeth Honeyborne, aged twenty-seven, showed what stern stuff she was made of. Despite having to make severe domestic economies, by 1802 she bought out her partners and subsequently ran Gothersley until 1811. We know from the Hodgson letters and cash books that the weekly wage bill was small, between £3 and £6. The mill by comparison with the South Wales and Black Country plants was insignificant, but her management of it was not. She paid casual labourers a shilling a day, whilst keepers were paid 21 shillings a week. She employed between four and eight men and Mr Cornforth was her manager. Wages fell off in the early autumn as the men returned home to gather in their harvests. Bills for coal amounted to between thirty and forty pounds a delivery. Other expenses included repairs to the pool dam and mill machinery, canal carriage and the buying in of grease (to oil the machinery), lime, coal and iron. Offsetting these expenses was the sale of rods and hoops (14). In 1811 she sold her shares in Aberdare and invested the money in government stock. Elizabeth leased Gothersley to Foster and Bradley for £110 per annum, whilst the value of the house was £56 per annum. The rent paid to Mrs Foley for the works and house had risen to £166 (15). She could now concentrate on running the farm.

In the course of time her daughter, Emma, married Henry Hodgson (1823) and as he showed a great interest in the works Elizabeth did not renew the lease with Foster and Bradley. Henry ran Gothersley until his failing eyesight forced him to retire in 1830 (16). After this George and Edward Thorneycroft took the lease. They were the first of many. In 1833 John Hunt and William Brown were there and within three years Joseph Maybury of Bilston was the lessee. In 1849 it was E B Dimmock and John Thompson of Bilston, whilst a further list of leaseholders included SW Bunn in 1861; Bunn and W Hatton; William Finnemore and Richard Titley; and Finnemore (17). It is clear that it was difficult to make a good profit at Gothersley during this period. The ironworks closed in 1890 and was offered for sale the following year.

The way that the Smestow was used to drive the machinery is interesting. As in many mills and forges upstream, the river itself was diverted to fill the mill pools. The old river bed was used as

a back brook, carrying any surplus water around the works. This was possibly to protect existing water rights and avoid litigation. A tributary stream, the Spittle Brook, joins the Smestow at Gothersley, a leat from which also fed the mill pools, whilst the brook itself was culverted under the Smestow and joined the Back Brook. Today the Smestow continues to flow in its new river bed on the west side of the valley; the Back Brook is a ditch with a little brackish water.

Fig. 102   Back Brook, Gothersley

Gothersley ironworks is an example of industrial inertia. It is surprising it lasted as long as it did, when reverses in the iron trade in the 1870s closed many a plant and when Gothersley was in competition with works on the coalfield, which had the advantage of cheap raw materials. However, Gothersley did have cheaper water

power and the canal as a lifeline for its supplies and exports. The land has been returned to agriculture and there is little visual evidence to show there was once an ironworks here. The circular canal-side toll house has been reduced to a few feet in height and there is still an overgrown cartway to the former works. The wharf for loading and unloading remains, and nearby on the opposite side of the canal is a weed-infested winding hole for turning boats – or is it an additional wharf where boats would lie up until it was their turn to unload or load?

Fig. 103   Remains of Roundhouse (toll house) on canal

Beyond Gothersley the Smestow valley is pinched by the slopes descending from Enville Common on the west and by the steep gradients of Colbourns Rough on the east. This is a particularly beautiful part of the valley, with the river twisting and turning in its attempt to reach the Stour at Devil's Den. The genius of Brindley, the canal builder, is evident as he somehow managed to fit the cut into this sylvan scene.

Fig. 104   Prestwood House (south-west elevation), 1913

Prestwood House and grounds lies above the Smestow and canal. Originally a hunting lodge in the Royal forest, it passed through the hands of several important families – the Sutton Dudleys; John, Duke of Northumberland; the Littletons; and the ironmaster family of the Foleys. Picturesque Prestwood remained in the hands of the Foley family until the entire estate of 4160 acres was put up for sale by Mr PH Foley in 1913. It comprised Prestwood House, Stourton Castle, Dunsley Hall, the Stewponey and Foley Arms and sixteen mixed farms. Prestwood's parkland was described as *'luxuriously timbered with fine forest trees and thriving plantations' (18)*. The house was redeveloped after a fire in the 1920s, and an imposing mansion was lost. For many years the hall and its adjacent buildings were a sanatorium and chest hospital. The wards were housed in three long low single-storey blocks. Its country location provided the fresh air and rest that were thought essential to combat tuberculosis, a disease that at one time was endemic in the Black Country *(19)*. There were also a number of sheds in the woods, which were used to isolate the most poorly patients. Many will remember the Sunday bus service provided by Midland Red to link in with the visiting hours. The Prestwood Hospital complex of 154 acres, comprising administration block, pavilion wards, nurses' accommodation, horticultural garden and glasshouses, tenanted farmland and woodland shoot was sold in 1985, by the West Midlands Regional Health Authority *(20)*. The coach house became a luxury courtyard development of twenty-seven independent units with nursing care provided. The house was turned into a nursing home *(21)*.

On the west bank of the Smestow is Prestwood pumping station, which began supplying water in 1927 to Shavers End reservoir in Dudley. It was a welcome addition to the South Staffordshire Water Company's capacity and went someway to meeting the conurbation's increasing needs. It was found that the groundwater was just five feet beneath the surface, showing what a valuable find this site was. Two boreholes were sunk (one of 568 feet and one of 531 feet) into the Lower Mottled Sandstone *(22)*. The station yields about 4.5 million gallons of water a day.

The Smestow River swings east to escape the confines of the hills in its attempt to join the Stour. Soon, it passes through an area of alder marsh known as Devil's Den. Above, on the east bank of the canal is a rustic and picturesque boathouse carved out of the red sandstone cliff. The punt which lay within once served the shooting parties at Prestwood, allowing them to cross the waterway, in their quest for pheasant, partridge, duck and snipe.

Fig. 105   The Boathouse, Prestwood

Shortly thereafter, the canal is carried on a two-arched aqueduct over the Stour, which began life on the slopes of the Clent Hills. Like the Smestow, this river once drove a succession of mills, forges and ironworks, including Prestwood, Stourton and The Hyde.

The Stour is one of six rivers in Britain carrying this name, and although pronunciation varies it means, from the Celtic, a river which is strong and powerful. Within a few yards of the aqueduct the Smestow reaches its goal, its waters swelling those of its neighbour, on their continuing journey to reach the Severn at Stourport.

Fig. 106   Canal aqueduct over the Stour

(1) Watermills and water-powered works on the River Stour, Worcestershire and Staffordshire part 5: Smestow Brook. SM Cooksey and MV Cooksey 1986. P16.

(2) The North Worcestershire Scythe Industry. PW King, 2007. P145. Historical Metallurgy Vol 41 Pt 2.

(3) A selection from the records of Philip Foley's Stour Valley iron works 1668-74. Pt 2. RG Schafer, 1990. P33. Worcestershire Historical Society Vol 13.

(4) Information from Mr Charles Wilkes, Checkhill Farm.

(5) ibid 3 P35.

(6) ibid 2.

(7) Victoria County History of Staffordshire Vol XX, 1984. P214.

(8) Information Mrs May Griffiths, the Wombourne Historian.

(9) Original agreement, "Terms and conditions for proposed railway from the Staffs and Worcs Canal to Shutt End, 27th January 1827". Author's collection.

(10) The History of the South Staffordshire Water Company 1853-1989.BV Williams and J Van Leerzem; Chapter3. Dudley Teachers' Centre.

(11) The Staffordshire and Worcestershire Canal. JI Langford, 1974. P134. Goose and Son.

(12) VCH Vol XX P147-8.

(13) Out of the Mahogany Desk. P54. KC Hodgson, 1971. P54. The Research Publishing Co. And: Gothersley Mill, R Davies, 1991. The Blackcountryman Vol 24 No. 2. P39.

(14) ibid 13 P61.

(15) ibid 13 P59-63.

(16) ibid 13 P63.

(17) ibid Davies R, P43.

(18) Prestwood Estate sale catalogue, July 1913. Edwards, Son and Bigwood.

(19) Prestwood. R Jones, 2010. See Blackcountryman Vol 43 No.3 for a patient's account.

(20) Tender document 'The Prestwood Hospital Complex', 1985. Allsop Sellers, 1 School St., Wolverhampton.

(21) Express and Star 21/2/90 Commercial feature.

(22) ibid 11 Chapter 4

Fig. 107   Confluence of the Smestow with the River Stour

The Smestow, its course full run, reaches the Stour at Devil's Den. But it is not truly finished, for its waters go to swell its cousin and ensure that it reaches Kidderminster and beyond. Eventually with the Smestow's help the River Stour will itself aid the mighty Severn as it travels to Gloucester and the Bristol Channel.

The Smestow is like a person, issuing forth into the world from the warm depths; growing stronger by the minute until its youth is passed and middle age increases its girth. With maturity comes old age and finally the end. But there is never an end – for as one flower dies another springs forth to take its place, and so too our children take up where we left off. It is just the same with each drop of water, in its ceaseless cycle: from falling rain to groundwater, to spring, rivulet, stream, brook, river and the sea, to evaporation, clouds, and rain again.

The Smestow Brook, Wolverhampton's River, has become South Staffordshire's River. It has been man's companion for many millennia and has provided him with a ready water supply, with river terrace sites for his home, with power to drive his mills to make flour, cloth and iron. Scythes and farm equipment have been fashioned in its forges and Civil War Royalists and Parliamentarians have taken their swords from its smiths. The cottage-based nail trade has been a part of the village scene in such settlements as Wombourne. Indeed, the Smestow has witnessed its own Industrial Revolution in the seventeenth and eighteenth centuries, when the Foleys integrated their commercial interests of blast furnace, forge and slitting mill, and all based on water power.

But most important of all is that the Smestow valley has provided and still provides many people of the Black Country with their clean water supply. This gift of life has been a pre-requisite of better health and better opportunity. Five waterworks line its or its tributaries' banks and extract up to fifteen million gallons daily from the pebble beds. The astute Henry Marten, a water engineer of the South Staffordshire Company, was expounding the Smestow Brook as a suitable supply in 1851 when he stated it could yield ten million gallons daily. William Butler knew of its potential, for he sited his brewery at Springfield and drilled boreholes to provide the water for his distinctive beers and ales.

Whilst it is claimed that the valley could provide twenty million gallons daily, water extraction has not been without cost. The water table has been lowered, with a resulting loss of water through the stream bed, making river flow less than it might have been. This is particularly true of the brooks flowing from Enville and for some of the minor tributaries, as well as for parts of the Smestow itself. However, the sewage plants at Trescott, Heathmill and Gospel End return clean water to the system. Their contribution is particularly valuable in summer months.

There is an abundance of wildlife across the Smestow drainage basin and we are the richer for it. Since the 1980s, with the loss of much heavy industry the Smestow has been cleaned up. The water voles and otters are back at least as far up as Smestow Bridge on the main river and as far as the Wodehouse House Pool on the Wom Brook. The kingfisher too is in evidence. This points to better fish stocks, and to a cleaner water quality supporting a wide range of flora and fauna.

In these days of energy conservation and the quest for renewables we don't seem to have explored the possibility of using water power to produce electricity along the Smestow system. Some of our forefathers produced electricity up until the Second World War at sites such as Checkhill and Wodehouse Mills. Given that schemes these days need to return a profit over time it may not be economic, but given that the water source is free it seems that a body like the Environment Agency might consider the Smestow system as a pilot scheme, which, if successful, could be rolled out over the country. The alternative is for the government to offer companies or individuals a grant to develop the potential which lies alongside their properties.

The Smestow Brook and River can and does flood. This is despite the extensive works carried out along its course over the last fifty years. Heavy and/or sustained rainfall in the conurbation runs quickly off the tarmac and concrete and causes rapid increases in river levels. Added to this is the rapid fall of some of the brooks from the South Staffordshire plateau, and it is little wonder that flooding can occur. The range of river level at Swindon is normally between 1.04 and 1.34 metres and yet it has been measured at 2.56 metres, twice the normal level range (1). At times like these it is worth avoiding Trescott or Longford or Bennett's Lane on the Smestow, Wom and Black Brooks respectively. As we seem increasingly prone to unpredictable weather patterns and suffer from flooding, perhaps we should look at ways of storing excessive water flow in the underground aquifer, thereby ensuring adequate stocks are available for extensive periods of little or no rainfall. The building of flood meadow dams would reduce flood risk and allow water to drain away naturally. The re-establishment of ponds could provide a water supply in case of forest fire as well as a scenic amenity and wildlife habitat. It is a matter of using our ingenuity to manage and protect scarce resources.

Whatever the pros and cons of the above, the Smestow Brook and its tributaries flow through some really lovely countryside.

Why not visit it today?

Fig. 108   The Smestow at Wightwick

(1) Environment Agency website - Smestow Brook at Swindon.

List of illustrations

Front cover images:

     View from junction of Withymere Lane and old Stourbridge Road (top left)
     Tunstall Water Bridge (top right)
     Disused mill wheel, Smestow Mill (bottom left)
     The Smestow at Wightwick (bottom right)

Back cover images:

     Tunstall Water Bridge
     Trysull Mill and yard, 1920s
     Ovens End bridge
     Mill Farm, Spittlebrook
     Great spur wheel, Mere Mill
     Enville Sheepwalks

Do you know the locations of each of the pictures that have been used in this book's chapter headings, plus the one on the dedication page?

Dedication   ....

Introduction   ....

Chapter 1   ....

Chapter 2   ....

Chapter 3   ....

Chapter 4   ....

Chapter 5   ....

Chapter 6   ....

Chapter 7   ....

Chapter 8   ....

Chapter 9   ....

Chapter 10   ....

Chapter 11   ....

Chapter 12   ....

Chapter 13   ....

Chapter 14   ....

Chapter 15   ....

Chapter 16   ....

Chapter 17   ....

Chapter 18   ....

Conclusion   ....